The Viola Da Gamba Its Origin And History Its Technique And Musical Resources

Nathalie Dolmetsch

THE VIOLA DA GAMBA

ITS ORIGIN AND HISTORY, ITS TECHNIQUE AND MUSICAL RESOURCES

No 759

NATHALIE DOLMETSCH

THE VIOLA DA GAMBA

ITS ORIGIN AND HISTORY, ITS
TECHNIQUE AND MUSICAL RESOURCES

HINRICHSEN EDITION LTD.

NEW YORK LONDON FRANKFURT ZURICH

Printed in England by Robert Stockwell Ltd , London, S E 1

Dedication

To the memory of my father, inspired pioneer
in the restoration of the music and instruments
of the sixteenth and seventeenth Centuries.

NATHALIE DOLMETSCH

5

CONTENTS

The Viola da Gamba

ITS ORIGIN AND HISTORY, ITS TECHNIQUE AND MUSICAL RESOURCES

by Nathalie Dolmetsch

TABLE OF ILLUSTRATIONS

CHAPTER I

ORIGIN AND EARLY HISTORY OF THE VIOL

IT is said that in the early years of the Christian religion, when the first Fathers founded the Church, they realized that it was not possible to make the populace abandon entirely their pagan credences, so to make the new beliefs easier for the people, the old gods were allowed to live on, in the subordinate positions of myth and legend. One who survived in this fashion was Orpheus, and with him his Lyre.

Clement of Alexandria, a Doctor of the Church who died in A.D. 217, was responsible for a decree by which a lyre was engraved on the rings worn by the Faithful. The lyre, by then no longer a living instrument, thus survived as a name and an emblem of divine music.

As the centuries passed, this legendary instrument gave the glory of its name to the early viol, and we find, in Italy, the Lyra da Braccio and the Lyra da Gamba; the first being played ' upwards,' held to the shoulder (as may be seen in many groups of angelic musicians, in Italian paintings) and the second ' downwards,' held between the legs, as its name implies.

The use of plucked musical instruments from the very earliest times has never been questioned; there is also a certain amount of evidence to suggest that the bow, fitted with horsehair, is of very ancient origin. Athanese Kircher (1602-80), a Jesuit who made exhaustive researches into music, the nature of sound, and many other branches of human knowledge, quotes, on the subject of the bow, one Schilte Haggiborim, a learned Hebrew author and commentator on the Talmud.

According to Haggiborim, the Instruments of the Sanctuary

were made in diverse fashions. They were thirty-six in number, and it was David who found the way in which each should be played. Amongst them were instruments called Neghinoth, made of wood, whose shape was rounded, with several holes in the back. They had three strings made of gut, from which the sound was drawn with a bow bound with the hair from the tail of a horse. Here is the passage as given by Kircher:

Neghinoth, suerunt Instrumenta lignea, longa & rotunda, & subtus ea multa formina; tribus fidibus constabant ex intestinis animalium, & cum vellent sonare ea, radebant fides cum Arcu compacto ex pilis caudae equinae fortiter astrictis.

Another instrument, he asserts, called Haghniugab, was just like a viola da gamba, and had six strings.

In Spain, another direct ancestor of the viol developed in later times, in company with a similar instrument which was plucked instead of bowed, and here it had the name of Vihuela; thus there existed side by side the plucked Vihuela de Mano and the bowed Vihuela de Arco. From this name derived the Italian Viuola and Viola, the Viula of Provence, the Viele of France (later Viole), and the English Viol. The name Viele became, in the sixteenth century, identified with the Hurdy-gurdy, which was, in fact, a kind of viol played with a wheel which rubbed on the strings, producing a bag-pipe like effect. In the twelfth-century Romance of Aucassin and Nicolette, it is recounted that Nicolette, in her search for Aucassin, disguised herself as a minstrel and travelled from country to country playing the Viele, until she finally discovered Aucassin at the English Court.

Another ancestor of the viol, to which it owes its sound-post, is the Celtic crwth. This instrument had a sound-post, attached to the foot of the bridge on the treble side, and going right through the sound-board to stand on the inside of the back. The tuning of the early viol, and also that of the two lyras, is related to that of the crwth.

An interesting picture in the Bible of Charles II (le Chauve) of France, who died in 877, shows David playing on a little triangular harp, surrounded by his four companions, each playing a different instrument. One of them, Heman, is plucking what appears to be a crwth.

Such crwths are also depicted on mediaeval manuscripts in England, Germany and the Low Countries. Also to be seen are instruments which appear to be vihuelas, generally plucked, but occasionally bowed. These have from four to six strings and are shaped like two circles one above the other, suggestive of the vihuela's modern representative, the guitar.

A 13th century monk, Jerome de Moravie, wrote in Paris a treatise which gives detailed particulars of the viol of his period. He states that the viol had greater freedom than the rebec, on account of its tuning which was in greater and lesser intervals (unlike the fifths of the three-stringed rebec). It had five strings and was tuned in two ways: the first, which he says was for modal music, was for a viol of which the bottom string (as on the crwth) was a drone and being outside the finger-board was not played on by the fingers. This drone was tuned to D below middle C. The next string (from the bass side) was tuned a fifth *below*, to G, with the third (and middle) string at the octave G above. The two upper strings were tuned in unison, to D above middle C. A different tuning became necessary for secular music and all cantus which required much movement, and the bottom string, no longer only a drone, needed to lie on the finger-board like the others. The other modification consisted in the fact that the top string, ceasing to be in unison with the second, was tuned to G above middle C.

Jerome mentions yet another manner of tuning but his meaning is obscured by a scribal error; it is clear, however, that the Drone D, had been abandoned, and the 'lowest' string on the bass side had now, in fact, become the lowest note on the instrument, tuned to G, like the second string of the previous tunings.

These tunings foreshadow the later developments of the viol in Italy, where it was to become two distinct instruments with their own sub-divisions. The first of these was the Lyra group (da Braccio and da Gamba) previously spoken of and which, retaining the drones, added considerably to its number of strings; the second, taking its name from the Spanish Vihuela and abandoning the drones altogether, evolved into the viola da gamba, with its immense possibilities for music of all kinds. The tuning, inherited from the vihuela side of its ancestry, became established in fourths, with a major third between the middle pair of strings, admitting of the playing in harmony in the manner of the lute and guitar, as was done in the sixteenth, seventeenth and eighteenth centuries.

The viola da gamba of the fourteenth and fifteenth centuries was a melodic instrument, suited to playing in concerted contrapuntal works, but not fitted for maintaining harmonies, for it had a narrow neck, which caused the strings to be close together on the finger-board and made it impossible to place the fingers cleanly on the notes of a chord without 'fouling' the other strings.

There is another member of the viol family, to which Michael Praetorius devotes a chapter in his " Syntagma Musicum " (1640); this is the Viola Bastarda. Praetorius describes it as resembling the tenor in sound (pitch?), which instrument it can replace in case of need, though the body, he tells us, is somewhat longer and larger. He can only guess at the origin of its name, though he suggests that it is probably a bastard from the other voices in the consort.

The viola bastarda was brought to England in about 1560, by Alfonso Ferrabosco I, and there it became popular under the name of Lyra Viol. Its part in the development of the viol is difficult to place and date. Praetorius states that (in the hands of a good master) it was able to maintain all the fugues and harmonies which were generally taken by a whole consort.

This relates it to one of its parents, the lyra da gamba, as does its English name; the Italian classification of it as *viola* bastarda gives, by implication, its other parent, the vihuela. This instrument and its technique will be dealt with in a later chapter.

In 1542, Silvestro Ganassi dal Fontego wrote a treatise on the viol, entitled " Regola Rubertina." In this work he warns the player against adopting " Moorish Attitudes," such as holding the viol crossways. This method of holding the viol relates it once again to the vihuela.

Ganassi's warning to the player also shows the strong Moorish influence on music in Spain (and from Spain to Italy), and suggests the possibility that he is quoting from an earlier work, that of his master, Ramon de Pareja, a Spanish Monk whose treatise, written in the previous century, has not survived.

The second volume of Ganassi's work is devoted to the bass viol, which he calls Violone: a viol with five strings. In this book he deals exhaustively with the method of testing strings to determine whether they are true or false, and the need for careful tuning both of frets and of the instrument. He tells the player that if after these precautions he finds his viol still out of tune when playing with others, his ear has obviously been at fault and he must try again to perfect himself.

Ganassi's violone is not the same instrument as that so named by Praetorius, which descended a fifth below the bass viol (down to GG) and was the Contra Basso da Viola of the 16th century.

At the close of the century, with the more general use of gut covered with wire for the lower strings (a new invention when Praetorius wrote his "Syntagma Musicum"), a true double-bass viol became possible a full octave below the consort bass.

In his second volume Ganassi also gives a description of viols mounted with only four strings, and others with three. Those with four were tuned with a third between the two lowest strings and a fourth between the others. The three-stringed instruments were tuned in fifths and were in fact, rebecs. Rebecs are also described by Martin Agricola under the name of Polische Geigen, in his rhymed treatise " Musica instrumentalis deudsch " (1545).

The viols of Agricola were of two kinds, the first, with six strings, he called Welsche Geigen, and the second, with only four strings, Kleine Geigen. These four-stringed instruments may have been, like the three-stringed rebec, ancestors of the violin, and have gifted it with a sound-post, which the rebec lacked.

The viol of the fifteenth century was a slim, graceful-looking instrument. Curved, but without corners, it had a waist which allowed the bow to move freely on the top and bottom string without touching the sides, and resembled the early guitar and vihuela, though in a more elongated form. The lyra da gamba, with its flat bridge intended to facilitate the playing of several strings at once, had not needed a waist, and such instruments frequently had ornamental outlines.

During the sixteenth century, the viol acquired corners, usually meeting " squarely," and without the extra " curl " which became standard on the violin, though a few basses were made with the violin outline.

The back was generally flat, though this was not invariable; there exist viols of all periods with shaped and rounded backs. The shoulders again were subject to variation; though usually sloping (which gave greater ease in reaching the end of the finger-board for playing in the higher positions), they were sometimes constructed to come in square to the heel of the neck, as on the violoncello, particularly on consort instruments.

The sound-holes on Italian viols were " F " shaped as on the violin (which points to an Italian origin for the violin's modern form), whilst those on English, French and German were "C" shaped, and occasionally on these latter, " flame " shaped. The Italian makers differed from those of other countries also on a point of construction. The tail-piece of their viol (to which the strings were attached) was fastened at the base by a thick piece of gut, looped round a button on the end of the instrument, as on the modern violin. The makers of other countries made a square hole through the tail-piece, through which a hook-shaped wooden peg was thrust, this being let-in and firmly glued in the base of the instrument.

Jean Rousseau, in his " Traité de la Viole " (Paris, 1687), tells us that though the viol is an instrument of great antiquity, it was in his time of comparatively recent introduction in France. His theory of its history in Europe is an interesting one; he places its origin amongst the Ancient Egyptians, though the instrument he describes is more related to the Eastern Rebec or Rhebab.

Rousseau asserts that the viol was handed from the Egyptians to the Greeks, from the Greeks to the Italians and from the Italians to the English, who were the first to compose and play pieces in harmony upon it. The English, he says, carried the knowledge of the viol to other kingdoms, and he names some of the musicians who were instrumental in doing this as: " Vvalderan " at the Court of Spain, "Joung"* with the Court of Innsbruck, " Pries " in Vienna and others in various places (allowance must be made for doubtful spelling of the English names).

The first viols in France, according to Rousseau, had five strings and were very large. The bridge was low and flat, and the thick strings tuned in fourths. The neck was heavy and upright, unlike the slim thrown-back neck of Rousseau's day. In time, a sixth string had been added, and later a seventh. For the seventh string Rousseau gives the credit to Mons. de St. Colombe, a celebrated violist of his time, to whom he also attributes the introduction of covered strings.

Another famous French player, the Abbé Maugars, spent four years in England at the Courts of James I and Charles I, from 1620 to 1624. There, he tells us, he gained much from

* William Young d. 1671.

those great English masters Giovanni Coperario (John Cooper) and Alfonso Ferrabosco II (born in Greenwich).

After Maugars' return to France, Mersenne wrote of him as follows, coupling him with another celebrated player, Hottman:

No one in France can equal Maugars and Hottman, both very skilled men in this art: they excel in divisions and by the incomparable delicacy and suavity of their bowing, above all when someone accompanies them on the Harpsichord. But the former also plays alone in two, three or more parts on the bass Viol with profuse ornamentation and a rapidity of fingers, about which he appears to concern himself so little, that nothing to compare with it has hitherto been heard from those who have played on the viol, or indeed any other instrument.

After leaving England, Maugars spent twelve years in the service of the Cardinal de Richelieu. This employment finished in 1636, in the following circumstances.

The Cardinal was giving a concert of music for voices at his Palace, with Louis XIII as the principal guest. Maugars, who was accompanying the voices on his bass viol, played with such vigour and brilliance as, in the King's opinion, to obscure the voices, and his Majesty sent him a message to that effect. " A plague on this ignoramus! " exclaimed Maugars angrily " I will never play before him again! " The King, as became a royal guest, laughed and pretended to be amused, but the Cardinal was greatly incensed, and very shortly procured Maugars' banishment.

From France, Maugars travelled to Italy; greatly to the benefit of music historians, as his letters from there give invaluable information as to the state of music in Italy at that time, and in particular as concerned the viol. In " Repons à un curieux sur le sentiment de la musique d'Italie " (1639) he wrote as follows:

The Lyra is still well esteemed among them, but I have not heard one player who can compare with Ferrabosco of England—as to the Viol, there is no one in Italy who excels on it, and indeed it is very little played in Rome: at which I am much surprised, seeing that formerly

PLATE No 1

CHAPTER No 1

Ganassi dal Fontego 'Regolo Rubertina,' 1542

SINGER ACCOMPAN'ED ON THREE FIVE-STRINGED VIOLS

PLATES Nos 2, 3

CHAPTER No 1

Dolmetsch Collection

BASS VIOLS WITH MORE THAN 200 YEARS BETWEEN THEIR CONSTRUCTION

Viol by Hans Volrat, Vienna (1475) showing the early outline without corners, and the narrow neck and fingerboard

A typical English Division Viol, by Barak Norman (1713) 'at The Bass Viol, in St Paul's Churchyard,' London

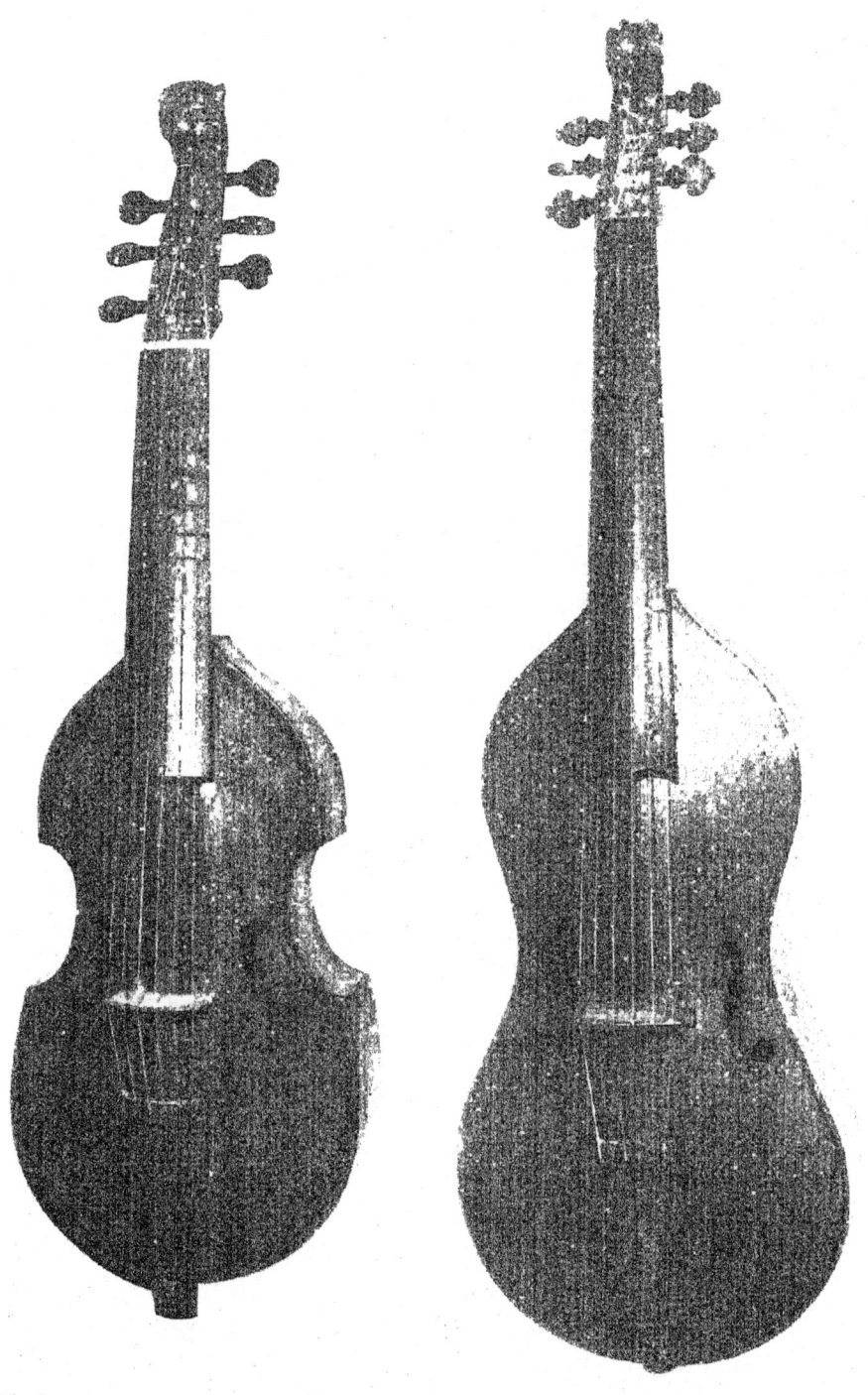

ENGLISH SEVENTEENTH CENTURY ALTO VIOL—ITALIAN TENOR VIOL, *ca* 1500

they had one Horatio de Parma, who did marvels on it and who left to posterity some excellent pieces, of which some of our people have made very good use on other instruments, as though they were of their own composing; and also the father of the great Ferrabosco, who brought the first use of it to the English [he is mistaken here, but perhaps he means as a solo instrument] *who then have surpassed all other nations.*

We learn that Maugars' playing was much admired by those who came to hear him privately in Rome, but that the professional musicians, jealous of a foreigner, remarked that it was all very well for him to play these elaborate solo pieces, and certainly they had never heard so many parts sustained on one viol, but that they doubted whether he would be capable of improvising divisions on a given theme. Maugars' answer was to arrange to give a public demonstration in the French Church in Rome, on the following day, which was the Feast of St. Louis. After the celebration of Mass, at which twenty-three Cardinals assisted, he mounted the rostrum with his viol, amid warm applause. He was then provided with a theme of some fifteen to twenty notes on which to improvise, accompanied on a small organ. This he did with such brilliance that he was entreated by the Cardinals to play again, after the Agnus Dei. This time he was given a rather gayer subject than the first, of which he wrote:

This I diversified with so many inventions and different kinds of movement and tempi, that they were greatly astonished and came to pay me compliments—This procured me the greatest honour which I ever received.

While the viol was in its decline in Italy, in England it was rising to its greatest musical heights, and was held in the highest esteem by musicians, both professional and amateur all over the country. Every large house had its " chest of viols," comprising generally a set of six, matched, instruments, preserved from damp in a large chest " lined with green baize " (such was the recommendation of Thomas Mace in " Musick's Monument," 1676).

Both consort and solo works were being composed and performed by such men as Alfonso Ferrabosco II, Richard Deering, Giovanni Coperario, William Lawes, John Jenkins, Christopher Simpson and many others.

Charles I maintained a private consort, at which the daring compositions of William Lawes must have obtained their first hearing. The King himself played the bass viol, having been, in his youth, a pupil of Ferrabosco II.

Oliver Cromwell, in his turn, maintained a consort, and he also played the bass viol. John Hingston, his organist, used to have concerts at his house, at which Cromwell was often present. A little anecdote comes to light in a pamphlet entitled " Truth and Loyalty vindicated " by Sir Roger L'Estrange, a Royalist who was to become one of the Licensers of published music under Charles II. This little story brings the musical picture of the times to life for us.

Being in St. James Park (writes Sir Roger), *I heard an organ touched in a little low room of one Mr. Hingston; I went in, and found a private company of five or six persons: they desired me to take up a viol and bear a part, I did so, and that a part too, not much to advance the reputation of my cunning. By and by, without the least colour of a design or expectation, in comes Cromwell. He found us playing, and as I remember so he left us.*

This happening led to other Royalists giving L'Estrange the appellation of " Noll's Fiddler," for they held that he should, on Cromwell's entrance, have laid down his viol and walked out. The story became so far distorted as to say that Sir Roger had managed to slip into the Protector's presence by bribing the servants, with a fiddle concealed under his cloak, and had then obtained a pardon by the charm of his playing. This it was which caused L'Estrange to publish his pamphlet, in 1662. " *Truly* " he added, " *my Fiddle is a Bass Viol, and that's somewhat a troublesome instrument under my cloak.*"

Though Cromwell supported a viol consort, and took delight

both in listening to the organ and to Deering's Latin motets, the Puritans degraded music by banishing it from the Churches and treating it, ultimately as a temptation of the Devil.

Some eminent musicians left the country; others, like Christopher Simpson, were maintained by their patrons.

Many Gentlemen of the Chapel Royal withdrew to Oxford, where consorts began to flourish in private, and music received a new impetus. Interesting accounts of some of the regular music meetings are given in the Musical Autobiography of Anthony Wood:

> *The gentlemen in private meetings, which A. W. frequented, played three, four and five parts with Viols, as Treble Viol, Tenor, Counter-Tenor and Bass, with an Organ or Virginal, or Harpsichon joyn'd with them: and they esteemed a Violin to be an instrument only belonging to a common Fidler and could not endure that it should come among them, for feare of making their meetings to be vaine and fidling. But before the Restoration of K. Ch. 2 and especially after, Viols began to be out of Fashion, and only Violins used, as Treble-Violin, tenor and Bass-Violin; and the King according to the French Mode, would have 24 Violins playing before him, while he was at Meales, as being more airie and brisk than Viols.*

Of the many musicians who met at the house of William Ellis, former organist of St. John's College, we hear interesting details; there were, for instance:

> *John Cock, M.A., Fellow of New Coll. by the Authority of the Visitors. He afterwards became Rector of Heyford-Wareyne near Bister and marrying one of the Woodwards of Woodstock, lived an uncomfortable life with her.—George Stradling, M.A., Fellow of Alls. Coll., an admirable Lutinist, and much respected by Wilson the Professor.—Ralph Sheldon Gent, a Rom. Catholick, admired for his smooth and admirable way in playing on the Viol—*

and many more; finally,

Proctor, a yong man and a new Commer—Proctor died in Halywell, and was buried in the middle of the Church there. He had been bred up by Mr. John Jenkyns, the Mirrour and Wonder of his Age for Music, and was excellent for the Lyra-Viol and Division Viol, good at the Treble-Viol and the Treble-Violin, and all comprehended in a man of three or 4 and twentie yeares of age. He was much admired at the Meetings, and exceedingly pittied by all the faculty for his loss [his early death].

——But when King Charles was restored the Episcopacy and Cathedrals with it, then did the Meetings decay, especially for this reason, because the Masters of Musick were called away to Cathedrals and Collegiate Choirs.

The viol consort as a composition, lingered on in England through the reign of James II and into that of William and Mary, with the consorts of Matthew Locke and Henry Purcell, though it is difficult, at this period, to place the dividing line between the works intended for viols and those for violins. The composers, sensitive to the changing trends and fashions, were writing in the vigorous, lively style considered appropriate to violins, though nevertheless possible on viols, and some works were published as suitable for either.

As a solo instrument, the bass viola da gamba was still in use in England, whilst in France it was at the height of its popularity. Marin Marais, Louis de Caix d'Hervelois and Antoine Forqueray were composing and playing their magnificent " Pièces " at the Court of Louis XIV. The " Pardessus de Viole " was also enjoying a period of expansion under de Caix d'Hervelois and lesser composers, and was accounted more suitable for young ladies than the violin.

In Germany, J. S. Bach was giving the gamba obbligati in cantatas, and sonatas with the harpsichord; G. P. Telemann was using it in duo and trio sonatas, and both were employing, with studied effect, the particular qualities of the instrument, such as its reedy clarity of tone and its capacity for playing in harmony.

Benedetto Marcello, in Italy, was writing his Sonatas for
" Violoncello o Viole di Gamba " (*sic*) with a continuo part for
the violoncello and harpsichord.

In 1740, the tide was already beginning to turn, and Hubert
le Blanc, in Paris, felt it necessary to write his little book " Defense
de la Basse de Viole contre les Entréprises du Violon et les
Prétentions du Violoncel." It was not until the close of the
century, however, that the viol really began to die out as a solo
instrument, and even then it was still considered by many to be
a better partner to the violin and harpsichord than the violoncello.

Jean Baptiste Forqueray (1700-83) and Karl Friedrich Abel
(1725-87) were the last great players of, and composers for the
viola da gamba. With its departure from the stage, the scene
was set for the violoncello in the string quartets and orchestras of
the nineteenth century.

PLATE No. 4a

**The Earliest Illustration
of a Viol by a European
Artist,** from a MS of the
Commentary of St Jerome on
the books of the Bible, written
at Canterbury. First part of
12th Century. Trinity College,
Cambridge (O.4.7.).

CHAPTER II

THE SIZES AND TUNINGS OF VIOLS

FROM the end of the fifteenth century the Viol and Violin families were established as of two distinct types of instruments: the first, fretted and generally tuned in fourths and one third, the second unfretted and tuned in fifths.

Writers from Virdung in 1511 onwards mention and describe both families of instruments. That of the Viola da Gamba will be considered exclusively here.

Virdung's Viol had nine strings and seven frets, and may have had a closer relationship to the Lyra da Gamba than the later instruments. Martin Agricola's Viols, in 1528, consisted of Treble and Tenor, with five strings, and Bass with six. The Bass was equivalent to the seventeenth century Tenor, tuned G, c, f, a, d, g, the third lying similarly between the middle pair of strings. The Tenor was tuned like the bass, but without the low G; the third, still between f and a, was no longer in the middle. The Treble, a fourth higher than the tenor, was tuned f, a, d, g, c, retaining the third between f and a as in the other Viols, thus bringing it between the lowest pair of strings (the tunings are all given here from the bottom up).

With Ganassi in 1542, "seventeenth century" tuning had become established, being both lower in the Bass and higher in the Treble, which now lay a fifth above the Tenor, which in turn being a fourth above the Bass gave an octave between the Treble and Bass.

> Ganassi: Treble d, g, c′, e′, a′, d″.
> Tenor   G, c, f, a, d′, g′.
> Bass   D, G, c, e, a, d′.

Ganassi mentions also a fourth member of the family, the Alto, which instrument in his time, though smaller than the tenor was tuned in unison with it.

Jean Rousseau in his " Traité de la Viole " (Paris, 1687) gives the following information. Having described the bass, he says:

There have been in use for some time three other viols of different sizes: one a little smaller than the Bass to serve as Tenor, and one a little smaller than the Tenor to serve as Alto; and finally one a little smaller than the Alto to serve as Treble. These four instruments take the parts of the four voices, as had been the practice in Italy long ago, where the four viols were tuned thus: the Tenor and Alto in unison, one fifth above the Bass (i.e. A to a') and the Treble one fourth above the Tenor and Alto, that is to say, one octave above the Bass (d to d").

When these four viols were used in France, the Tenor was tuned a fourth above the Bass [G to g'], the Alto a fourth above the Tenor [c to c"], and the Treble one tone above the Alto, at the octave above the Bass [d to d"].

Mersenne, in his " Harmonie Universelle " (1627) places the third on the alto between the 4th and fifth string (he counts from the top) giving f and a, in the following words:

As to the Haute-Contre [Alto] its tuning differs only from that of the others in that the 3rd and the 4th string give a fourth and the 4th and 5th string a major third—Since it is customary to tune the four recognised sizes of Viol together from the A, which is taken on the second string of the Treble and the Bass, on which one regulates usually all the Viols—

With the five-stringed altos, which are as numerous as the six-stringed, the top c" is missing, which makes them equivalent to a small tenor without the bottom G and they are well suited with the third between f and a.

In the consort-writing of such composers as Giovanni Coperario, Thomas Lupo, William Lawes, William White and Matthew Locke, there is frequently to be found a part from which its tessitura appears to have been written for an alto. This part is usually in the clef with " c " on the line next to the bottom (as is sometimes used for treble parts), instead of on the middle line of the stave as for the tenor. Certain instruments surviving from this period, large for a treble but small for a tenor, lend colour to the belief that the alto was used in England as well as on the Continent. It must be borne in mind, however, that it is not mentioned in the treatises of John Playford (1674) and Thomas Mace (1676). The addition of another "voice," or colour of sound to the complex works of the mid-seventeenth century is attractive, and useful in lightening involved contrapuntal passages, and a set of 2 Trebles, 1 Alto, 1 Tenor, 2 Basses makes a fine Chest of Viols for this period.

The size of each member of the family may vary considerably, as can be judged by the table which follows. The string lengths suggested are those that suit the size of body, and though best suited to a pitch of a semitone (approximately) below the modern "normal," are nevertheless able to come up to " diapason normal " (a=440) with strings of average thickness. For a pitch of another tone below, the string length should, ideally, be increased by the space of the two widest frets, making one tone, though the thickness of the strings is also useful in adjusting the pitch.

To the table has been added those extremes of the Viol family which are not generally used in the consort: the Pardessus de Viole and the Violone; the first known by its French name as most popular in that country and the second by its Italian name for the same reason.

The Pardessus, lying a fourth above the treble, though keeping its third between the c′ and e′, had either five or six strings. An interesting little pardessus in the " Historiska Museet " in Stockholm has seven strings and is tuned like a treble, with an added top g″.

The continental bass acquired an extra string at the bottom in the mid-seventeenth century, a low AA.

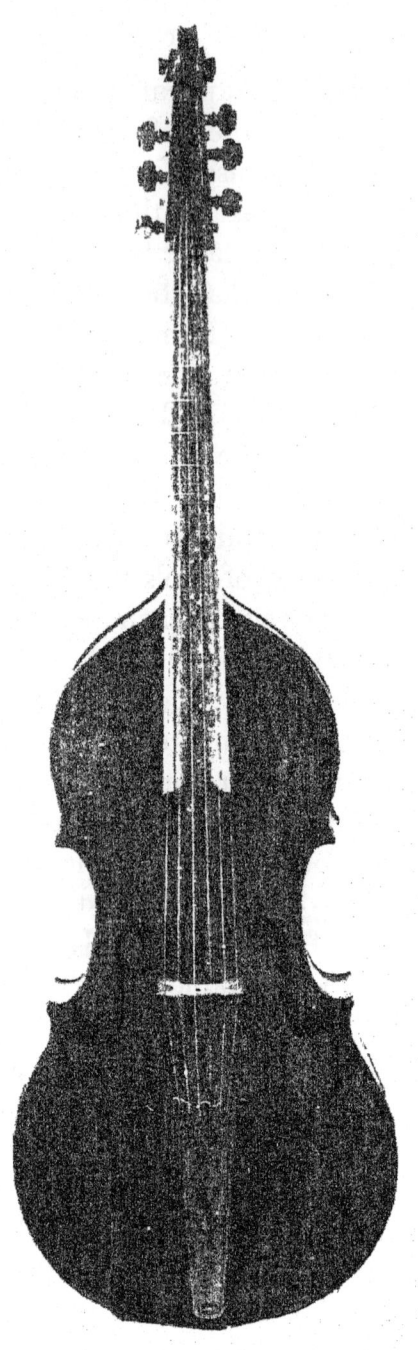

PLATE No 5   *Institut für Musikforschung, Berlin*
CHAPTER No 2

FIVE-STRINGED PARDESSUE DE VIOLE
by Paul-François Grosset, Paris (1742)

PLATE No 6   *Dolmetsch Collection*
CHAPTER No 2

FULL-SIZED VIOLONE
by Giovanni Paolo Maggini, Brescia (1580-1632)

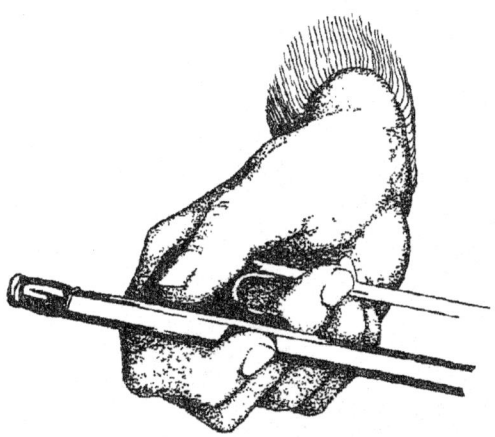

Position of hand and wrist at beginning of
forward (accented) stroke, to be maintained for
⅗-¾ of bow, at which point arm is stopped, hand
and wrist continue stroke.

Position of hand and wrist at beginning of
backward (pulling) stroke to be maintained for
⅗-¾ of bow, after which arm stops, hand and
wrist travel back (' closing ' the hand)

Left hand placed on bass or tenor, with rounded
wrist, fingers immediately behind frets, and thumb
grasping neck opposite second finger

PLATE No 10   *Simpson 'Division Viol' (1667)*
CHAPTER No 3

HOW TO HOLD VIOL AND PLACE HANDS

PLATE No 11
CHAPTER No 3

HAND AND FINGERS HOLDING BOW OF MODERATE LENGTH
Detail from ' The Family of Jacques van Eyk ' by Gonzales Coques (1614-84)

Variations in the Sizes of Viols

	length of body		*length of string (bridge to nut)*	
PARDESSUS DE VIOLE (g), c′, e′, a′, d″, g″	12⅜″ 31.5 cm.	—12⅝″ —33 5 cm.	12⅝″ 33 cm.	—12⅞″ —33.5 cm.
TREBLE VIOL (Dessus de Viole, Diskant) d, g, c′, e′, a′, d″	13¾″ 35 cm	—15″ —39 cm.	13¾″ 35 cm	—14″ —35 5 cm.
ALTO VIOL (Alto, Alt) c, f, a, d′, g′ (c″)	15″ 35 cm	—16″ —41 cm	15″ 35 cm.	—15⅞″ —40.5 cm.
TENOR VIOL (Taille, Alt-Tenor) (G), c, f, a, d′, g′	18½″ 47.5 cm	—20¾″ —53 cm.	17½″ 45 cm	—21½″ —52 cm.
(Note that the smaller Tenors are usually without bottom G)				
LYRA VIOL variable tuning	21¾″ 55.5 cm.	—23¾″ —60 cm	21″ 53.5 cm.	—23¾″ —60 cm.
DIVISION VIOL (Viola da Gamba) D, G, c, e, a, d′	24¼″ 62 cm.	—26¾″ —68 cm	25½″ 65 cm.	—26″ —66 cm.
BASS VIOL OR CONSORT BASS (Viola da Gamba, Basse de Viole) (AA), D, G, c, e, a, d′	26½″ 68 cm.	—27¾″ —71 cm.	26½″ 68 cm.	—27½″ —70.5 cm.
VIOLONE DD, GG, C, E, A, d	38⅝″ 98 5 cm.	—39½″ —105 cm	38″ 97 cm.	—39½″ —105 cm.

*

CHAPTER III

THE FIRST ESSENTIALS OF
VIOLA DA GAMBA TECHNIQUE

THOMAS MACE, who, in his " Musick's Monument " (1676)
gives a considerable amount of useful advice on playing the
viol, precedes it with remarks on the instrument the player
should choose:

> First [says he] *make Choice of a Viol fit for your Hand; yet
> rather of a scize something too Big than (at all) too little (Especially if
> you be young and Growing).*

The technique of the viola da gamba, unlike that of members
of the violin family, varies very little through the range from
treble to bass, as all sizes are held downwards between the knees,
and bowed " under-hand." It is therefore easy, if the player so
wishes, to change from one to another as the hand becomes larger.
Roger North, the seventeenth century musical historian writes in
his autobiography that, as a boy, he was a pupil of John Jenkins
for the treble viol, changing to the bass as a young man at
Cambridge.

Members of the viol family are fretted, like lutes and guitars,
the only exceptions to this rule being the viole d'amore, which, as
they are played up, like the violins, are viole da braccio and not
viole da gamba.

Christopher Simpson in " The Division Viol " (1659),
describes the strings and frets as follows:

> It [the viol] *must be accommodated with six Strings; and with
> seven Frets, like those of a Lute, but something thicker. If also you
> fasten a small Fret, at the distance of an Octave from the open Strings*

32

(which is the middle betwixt the nut and the Bridge) it will be a good Guide to your Hand, when you stop that part of the Finger-board.

The frets give to the viol its characteristic clarity of tone, brilliant in solo music and essential to the clear performance of the close counterpoint in the consorts. Each note, coming off the fret, has much of the brightness of the open string coming off the nut. The frets, being of gut tightly tied with a special knot ideally suited to the purpose, are tunable by the player. It is also possible to tune in playing, by pushing or pulling the string with the finger.

John Playford in " A Brief Introduction to the Skill of Music " (1658) advises as to the bow to be used:

In the choice of your Bow, let it be proportioned to the Viol you use, and let the Hair be laid Stiff and the Bow not too heavy.

The bow of Playford's day was more commonly one with a fixed nut; the tightness of the hair being therefore regulated by the maker. An adjustable nut should be screwed-up so that the stick forms a slight outward " bow," and the hair is " laid stiff."

Jean Rousseau, in his " Traité de la Viole " (Paris, 1687), has much to say concerning the height of seat to be employed:

The first point to be considered for placing the viol is to take a convenient seat, neither too high nor too low: it is not necessary, however, for all those who play the viol to subject themselves to this rule: for one must accustom oneself to play on all kinds of seats—but it is certain that in the beginning it is good to use a convenient one.

The position of the viol when it is to be played is described by Playford as follows:

In holding your viol observe this Rule, place it gently between your knees, resting the lower end thereof upon the calves of your legs, and let your feet rest flat on the ground; your toes turned a little outward, and let the top of your viol lean towards your left shoulder.

Further details as to the position may be gathered from Thomas Mace:

Then enter into your posture; which is Thus. Having placed yourself on such a convenient Seat for Height, and in a Comely, Upright, Natural Posture; so as your knees may not hinder the Motion of your Bow, by Bending; set your Viol Down between the Calves of your Legs and Knees; so as by them, it may stand steadily, without the help of your Left Hand, and so fast that a stander-by cannot easily take it from Thence.

Certain points which have not been made clear by Playford or Mace, are clarified by Rousseau, who states that the player must sit on the edge of the seat, so as to be able to play more freely, and " d'une manière plus degagée "; that the viol must be carried with the left hand at the " heel " of the neck, close to the body of the viol and not by the middle of the neck, which might disturb the frets, " comme il arrive assez ordinairement "; and that the actual height of the viol between the calves of the legs will vary with the size of the players, the height of the seat and the size of the instrument.   He has a little more to add about the positions of the feet, which, he says, should be turned out, the left a little more, and a little further forward than the right; always kept flat on the ground and never turned on their sides or with the heel off the floor.

It can be further observed from contemporary paintings, that the viol was not allowed to rest against the player's shoulder, but was held well away, balanced in a comparatively upright position.

The viol being well placed, Mace continues with instructions for holding the bow:

Then take your Bow betwixt your Right Thumb, and two Fore-Fingers, near the Nut; the Thumb and 1st Finger Fastening upon the Stalk, and the 2nd Finger's-End Turned in Shorter against the Hairs; by which you may Poyze, and keep up the Point of your Bow; but if that Finger be not Strong enough, joyn the 3d Finger in Assistance to It; but in Playing Swift Divisions, 2 Fingers and the Thumb is Best.

He adds ingenuously:

This is according to Mr. Simpson's Directions.

Yet I must confess, that for my own Part, I could never Use It so well, as when I held it 2 or 3 inches off the Nut (more or less) according to the Length or Weight of the Bow, for Good Poyzing of It; But 'tis possible, that by Use I might have made It as Familiar to My self as It was to Him.

This difficulty is readily understood when it is realised that during the sixteenth century, the viol bow had become progressively longer as the makers attempted to gratify increasingly, the players' desire for a long stroke. This, as may be seen from Mace's words, defeated its object, as it was not possible to balance such bows except by holding them two or three inches off the nut.

There are some good illustrations of the position of hand for holding a bow of moderate length in contemporary paintings. One, by Domenico Zampieri (1581-1641) represents St. Cecilia playing on a small double-bass viol or violone, while a cherub holds up her music. Another, of comparatively late date, shows a young man playing on a six-stringed viola da gamba; this is by Gonzales Coques (1614-1684) and portrays the "Family of Jacques Van Eyck." A clear picture of a very long bow, and the manner of holding it, can be seen in the engraved portrait of Johann Schenk I, by his brother Peter Schenk. Johann was a virtuoso German viola da gambist of the late seventeenth and early eighteenth centuries.

In the management of the bow, the general consensus of opinion seems to have been that the long stroke should come from the shoulder, assisted at the end by the wrist, and the short stroke entirely from the wrist. The elbow should play no part in the movement, though stiffness is to be avoided. In the words of Rousseau:

To manage the bow, the wrist must be advanced inwards [with the hand thrown back] and, beginning to push the bow from the end, the wrist must follow, yielding: which is to say that the hand must

35

advance inwards, and when one pulls the bow back one must carry the hand outwards, following the arm without pulling the elbow; for one must not advance it on the forward stroke nor take it back on the backward one [the elbow].

And, to quote Mace:

So likewise, for the Exact straitness of the Bow-Arm, which some do contend for, I could never do so well, as with my Arm (Straight enough yet) something Plying, or Yeilding to an Agile Bending: which I do conceive most familiarly Natural.

For I would have no Posture Urg'd, Disputed, or Contended for; that should Cross, or Force Nature.

Now being thus far ready for exercise [continues Mace] *attempt the striking of your Strings; but before you do that, Arm yourself with Preparative Resolutions to gain a Handsome-Sweet-Smart-Clear-Stroak; or else Play not at all: for your Viol be never so Good, if you have an Unhandsom-Harsh-Rugged-Scratching-Scraping-Stroak, (as too many have) your Viol will seem Bad, and your Play Worse.*

Under the marginal heading: " The surest way to gain a Sweet Stroke " Mace states:

Only to draw your Bow just Cross the Strings in a Direct Line, endeavouring to Sound one Single String, with a long Bow, well-nigh from Hand to Point, and from Point to Hand Smoothly, and not Dripping, or Elevating the Point in the least.

This is the First and Best Piece of Practice you can follow; and till you have gain'd This, think of Nothing else.

Speaking of the Division Viol, Simpson advises:

I Told you before that you must stretch out your Arm Streight, in which posture (playing long notes) you will necessarily move your shoulder Joint; but if you stir that Joint in quick Notes, it will cause the whole body to shake; which (by all means) must be avoyded; as also any other indecent Gesture. Quick Notes therefore must be express'd by moving some Joint nearer the Hand; which is generally agreed upon to be the Wrist.

Mace further explains that this movement begins and ends the long strokes, and describes it as " a further jet of the wrist."

Rousseau urges the importance of using long strokes of the bow, and besides advising the use of one finger on the bow-hair, gives the information that the bow should lean downwards towards the bridge.

The instructions of all these masters, coupled with the information gained from contemporary paintings, can be précised as follows:

The bow should be grasped between thumb and first two fingers. The thumb, on a bow of moderate length (not exceeding 24 ins. bow-hair " playing " length) lies across the nut; correspondingly across the stick on a longer bow. The first finger is curled aslant over the stick, and the tip of the second finger pressed firmly on the bow-hair.* The palm of the hand is turned a little upwards, and this with the help of the thumb, balances the bow. The bow is tipped downwards towards the bridge, so that it rests on the edge of the hair. The forward, accented stroke, " poussez," begins at the point, with the hand bent back from the wrist, bringing the palm close to the bow-hair. The arm pushes the bow from the shoulder, for three-quarters of the stroke. At this point the arm stops and the hand continues to go forward from the wrist, to finish the stroke. The hand remains in this extended position, with the wrist quite loose and relaxed, for three-quarters of the return stroke, " tirez," while the arm pulls back the bow from the shoulder. The last quarter is accomplished by the wrist, the hand recovering its original position.

Simpson and Rousseau agree that the bow should cross the strings at a distance of two or three inches from the bridge. Mace tells his reader that:

If it be a Large-Consort-Viol, your Bow must Move about 2 Inches and a Half from the Bridge; if a Treble-Viol, about an Inch and a Half; and so upon all Others, according to This Suitable Proportion.

---

* The 3rd finger may be joined to the 2nd, some players prefer this.

Rousseau gives his readers an idea of the quality of sound that the viol bow should be expected to produce. He is speaking of Mons. Hottman, who, he says, was the first to compose, in France, pieces in harmony realized upon the viol, and the first to produce " de beau chants " which imitated the voice, in such that one admired him often more in the tender performance of " une petite chansonette " than in the fullest and most learned works.

The tenderness of his play [says Rousseau] *came from these beautiful strokes of the bow which he animated and softened with such skill and judgment that he charmed all those who heard him, and this it is which began to give perfection to the viol, and to make it be esteemed above all other instruments.*

The position of the left hand and arm are also well described by the writers already quoted.

You must not [says Simpson] *grasp the neck of your Viol like a violin; but rather (as those that Play on the Lute) keep your thumb on the back of the Neck, opposite to your fore-finger; so as your Hand may have liberty to remove up and down, as occasion shall require.*

On the subject of fingering Simpson states:

When you set any Finger down, hold it on there; and play the following Notes with other Fingers, until some occasion require the taking it off. This is done as well for better order of Fingering, that the Fingers may pass smoothly from Note to Note, without lifting them too far from the Strings, as also to continue the Sound of a Note when the Bow has left it.

In discussing the position of the left hand Rousseau speaks of St. Colombe, the pupil of Hottman, who, he asserts, even surpassed his teacher:

—for besides the beautiful strokes of the bow which he learnt from Mons. Hottman, it is from him in particular that we have the fine carriage of the hand which has given the last perfection to the viol, has made performance easier and free-er, and made it possible to imitate all the most beautiful ornaments of the voice, which is the only model of all the instruments.

PLATES Nos 12, 13
CHAPTER No 4

Rousseau 'Traité de la Viole' (1687)

THE RULES OF BOWING

Left, Rousseau's example, right, the same marked according to his directions
'V' indicates point of bow, '⊓' indicates heel, or square end of bow ('Example'
is in bass clef, for a 7-stringed Viol)

PLATE No 14
CHAPTER No 4

*Domenico Zampieri
(1581-1641)*

ST CECILIA PLAYING ON A SMALL VIOLONE

The hands show a graceful, relaxed hold, the right hand is in the 'pulling' position for a backward stroke

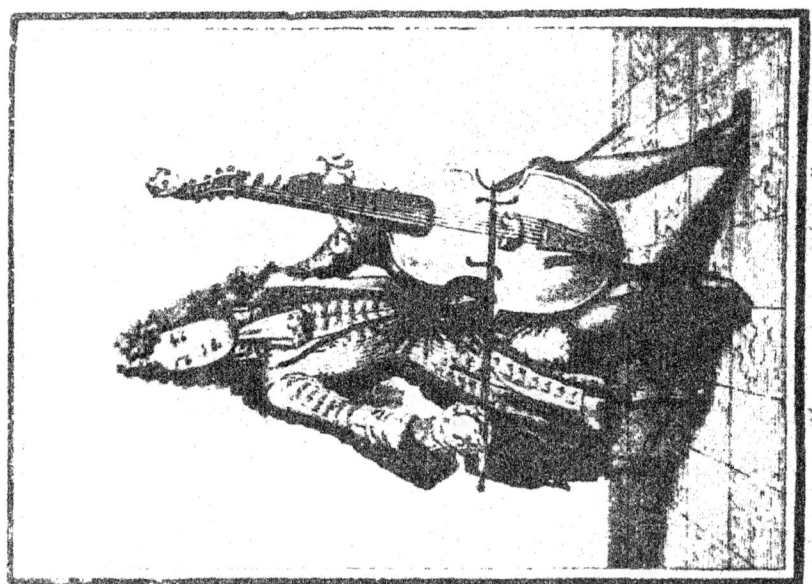

PLATE No 15
CHAPTER No 5

FRENCH ENGRAVING

of gentleman, playing on a small seven-stringed Viola da gamba, with ten frets
He is leaning it forward to draw on the lower strings, a useful practice

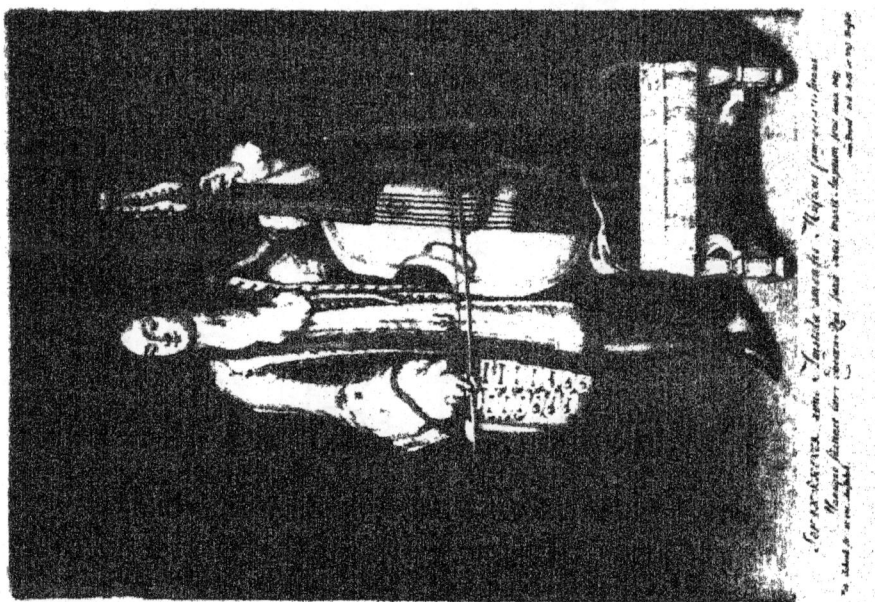

PLATE No 16
CHAPTER No 5

JOHANN SCHENK, A CELEBRATED GERMAN VIOLA DA GAMBA PLAYER

from an engraving by his brother Peter Schenk, of about 1700
Note the extremely long bow, and method of holding it.

EXEMPLE.

Comme s'il y avoit.

Example of ornamentation from Rousseau 'Traité de la Viole' (1687) the plain
version above, the ornamented below. Trills indicated by Rousseau with a cross
(letters on lower example, not on original) have been added for clarification

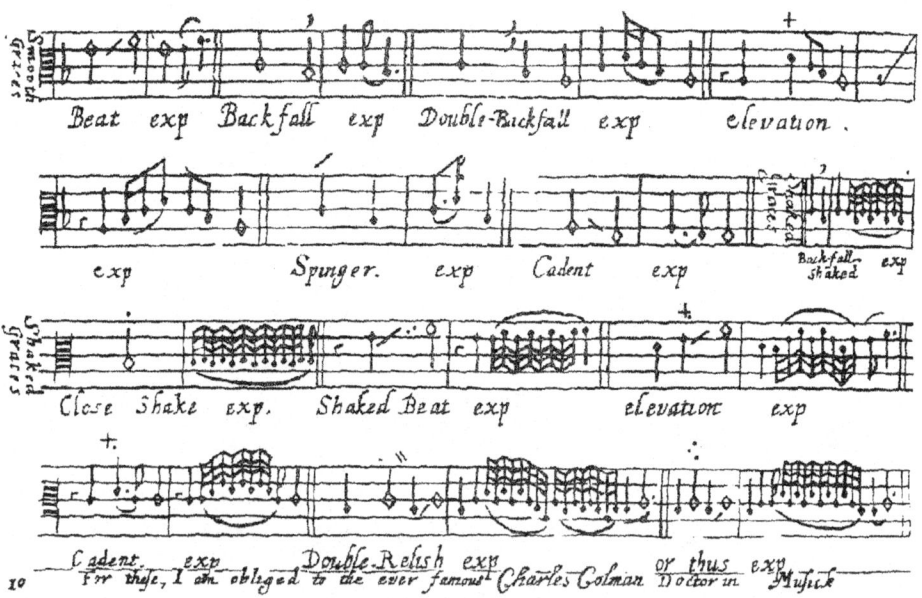

PLATE NO 19
CHAPTER NO 6

Charles Colman's Table of Ornaments, from Christopher
Simpson's Division Viol,' 1667

PLATE NO 20
CHAPTER NO 6   MARIN MARAIS
holding his large seven-stringed Viola da gamba across his knee

In speaking of the position for holding the viol, he points out that it must not be supported by the left hand, for this must be free to move, and even to remove the thumb when practising vibrato. The viol, he tells us, should be held firmly between the legs, as otherwise it would risk falling against the shoulder.

Further guidance is to be obtained from that great master of the viol, Marin Marais. In the preface to his first book " Pièces à Une et à Deux Violes " (Paris, 1686) he writes:

> *The carriage of the hand, which gives all the grace and facility of performance, consists in rounding the wrist and the fingers; in not hollowing the hand; and in placing the thumb opposite the middle finger, by this agreeable position of hand, the fingers reach all the chords naturally.*

It will be observed that the French writers advise that the thumb should be opposite the middle finger, whereas the English place it opposite the first finger. There may be a slight advantage in the French method for holding chords, though this is debatable.

Accurate information as to the spacing of the fingers of the left hand, on the bass and division viol, is to be found in many of the works already quoted. The fingers are placed on the tips, firmly pressed immediately behind the frets, so that the fret can be felt; the first finger behind the second fret, the second finger behind the third, and so on, one to a fret. This is the starting place for a novice; from here the first finger should extend back to the first fret when this is required, and sometimes the whole hand moves back into this " half-position," for ease of fingering in certain passages.

Further information as to fingering will be found in the next chapter.

Another work which should be mentioned is that of Danoville, published in 1686, entitled " L'Art de toucher le Dessus et la Basse de Viole, contenant tout ce qui est necessaire, d'utile et de curieux dans cette Science." This little " Avertissement," as Rousseau calls it, covers part of the same ground as Rousseau's " Traité de la Viole " though in less detail.   The author undertakes that the beginner who follows his method shall learn to play in six months.

Though Rousseau, in his work, attacks Danoville on a number of small points (without actually naming him), Danoville's advice is generally sound, and in line with Rousseau's.   He warns the beginner:

—to abstain from making grimaces, such as gestures of the head, openings of the mouth, and movements of the body, which are postures that generally displease everyone.

The spacing of the left hand on the treble viol is another point on which Danoville is informative.   Though he does not give actual fingerings, he speaks as follows:

The distance between the frets of the Bass determines that the fingering which suits it does not also suit the Treble.   The difference is to be seen in pieces that are full of chords, composed by various authors, for the performance of which they are obliged to mark fingerings. That is to say, that when it is the first finger they mark a figure 1, above the necessary note to be played, and similarly the other fingers, sometimes a 2, a 3, or a 4—The Treble rejects this method, because use of all the fingers makes the accuracy of the notes difficult to achieve.   The distance between the frets is too little and too constricted, which causes the fingers to have as much difficulty in being compressed as they have in being extended on the Bass—

CHAPTER IV

THE RULES FOR BOWING

THE elements of bowing, so fully described by the old masters have been laid down in the previous chapter. The theory behind them, and the practical necessity for using the wrist at the end of the stroke are readily appreciated if an experimental stroke is made with an entirely stiff wrist; it will be observed that the bow moves in a curve, skidding on the string. In the normal bowing the wrist compensates for this natural curve by its movement, towards the end of the stroke, which keeps the bow moving in a straight line. This is essential to a clear pure tone.

The leaning of the bow, so that the edge of the hair first touches the string, gives a light attack, and is also done, as Rousseau tells us:

—so that the hand may carry itself naturally and not be constrained.

The rules here to be set out concern the direction of the bow, according to the accents required in the music. The fact that the viol by its nature and its type of bowing, is not expected to give strong, hard accents, lest it should depart from its own character and imitate the violin, still leaves the need to use the bow in the correct direction, if the composer's intentions are to be carried out. The principle must be grasped that with the "underhand" bowing of the viol, the accented stroke is the forward one, that is to say the stroke which begins with the point of the bow on the string, and with the hand at the farthest distance from the string.

Direction of the bow was one of the things which Marin Marais considered important enough to mark, wherever there was the least occasion for doubt, so that his works might be correctly interpreted. He employed a small " p " for the forward stroke called " poussez " (push) and a small " t " for the backward stroke " tirez " (pull).

Though a perpetual correction of bow direction by quick adjustments is both unnecessary and fidgety, a little care can ensure that the important notes are on the strong, forward stroke.

Speaking of the bow Rousseau says:

If the Viol, played by the left hand with all the graces, is a body, one can say that the bow is the soul, since it brings and expresses all the passions which can be expressed by the Voice and which distinguish the various tempi of a melody; which is why it is of great consequence to use the bow according to the rules, and further proof of this necessity is the exactness with which the Masters mark the bowings in their pieces.

Further one knows that it is one of the things which set the difference between the Viol and the Violin; that the bowing is exactly opposite, and that you must push on the Viol what you pull on the Violin, and push on the Violin what you pull on the Viol. The reason for this difference is that in Viol playing, the strength of the arm is in pushing, and with the Violin it is in pulling, on account of the different manner of holding these two instruments, and it is also for this reason that on the Viol one pushes the longs and pulls the breves; which is done in contrary fashion on the Violin.

Rousseau gives a chart with various time signatures and phrases, following each other in musical sequence, and a series of lettered instructions for bowing them. This is most valuable, though he has made them a little confusing to follow by changing the order of the alphabetical references on the musical examples. Once this is realized the bowings will be found to accord with those here added to a duplicate of Rousseau's chart.

The instructions are quoted in full as they are of general application.

At the sign of Common time, or of four Beats [in the bar], when one finds Crotchets, of which the first is the first or third part of a Bar one must begin with a forward stroke, even though the number of notes of equal value should be uneven A, and if it is the second or fourth part of the Bar one must take a backward stroke B.

At the same time signature, when one finds Quavers, and the first is the first part of a Beat one must use a forward stroke C, & if it is the second part of a Beat, one must use a backward stroke D.

At the same Signature, when one meets Semi-quavers, & the first is the first or third part of a Beat one must use a forward stroke E, and if it is the second or fourth part of a Beat you must use a backward stroke F.

When in the course of a Piece of Music one meets, with a backward bow, Quavers of which the first is the first part of a Beat, one must use a back stroke for the first and the second G, & if one meets Semi-quavers with a backward bow, of which the first is the first or third part of the Bar, one must equally use a back bow for the first and second H, this rule must be observed in all Time Signatures.

If in the course of a Piece there occurs a descending coulé [of a third] or a final Cadence of which the last note is long enough to recover the bow, one should observe the bowing rules as at the beginning of a Piece I.

When one slurs an Octave, or some Passage with a single [back] stroke of the Bow, one must always use a forward stroke for the landing note of the Octave or Passage K.

It must be mentioned here that there is a difference between slurring the notes and drawing them. In slurring only the fingers move, & the Bow must not leave the strings: In drawing twice, the Bow should be lifted about half way through the stroke and replaced immediately to continue the stroke without starting it again.

When one finds Quavers or Semi-quavers of which one is obliged to draw the first and second in accordance with the foregoing Rule; if the Tempo is a quick one, the bow should not be raised, but the notes slurred with a single stroke.

In Pieces of Music where the Tempo is very quick (leger) one usually allows the Bow to take its course, when one has observed the rules at the beginning; for with regard to what may follow, one does not observe the *Rules* of which we have spoken, unless one meets notes long enough to favour the bowing.

In *Triple Time*, if the first *Bar* is composed of three notes of a *Beat* each, you must begin with a backward stroke L. And if the first is worth two beats, or if it is dotted, you must begin with a forward stroke M.

It follows that if the *Piece* is *Lively*, with accents on the first *Note* of each bar on *Notes* worth one beat, if the first two notes are the same [in pitch] one should use a forward stroke on the first and draw the next two backwards without raising the bow; that is to say marking the second at the half whilst continuing the same stroke N. But if the first and second of the *Bar* are on different notes, they must be played with a single forward stroke; which is to say that at the half of the *Forward* stroke the second *Note* should be marked whilst continuing the stroke O. This rule must be observed particularly when the *Notes* rise or fall by degrees, & it must be noted that I am speaking of *Quick Music.*

For the same time *Signature* when the *Piece* calls for no accent on any *Beat* of the *Bar*, and that it moves always evenly, the *Bow* should be allowed to take its course P, unless one should encounter some *Pauses*, or some final *Cadence*, or in fact some other *Note* long enough to favour the bowing without affecting the *Piece* (*Mouvement*).

At the same *Sign for Triple Time*, when one finds a *Note* worth two *Beats* at the beginning of the *Bar*, in the course of a *Piece*, with a *Backward Bow*, if it is followed with a *Note* of a single *Beat*, it must be taken with a back bow, that is to say with a continuation of the same stroke, slightly lifting the *Bow*, as we have said before Q.

At the same *Time Signature*, if each *Bar* is mixed with crotchets and minims which syncopate in rising, one should follow the bow, and when this *Mixture* ceases one begins again to observe the *Rules* R.

In *three-eight Time* the bowing of the *Quavers* should be performed as one observed for the *Crotchets* in *Triple Time*.

In all *Time Signatures*, when one meets a dotted *Crotchet* or *Quaver* with a back stroke one must take the following *Note* with the same Bow, as much as the Time permits, and note that I mean a dotted Crotchet or Quaver in Common Time to rule [as an example of] the other values of Notes in other Time Signatures S.

In six-four Time, one must follow the same Rules as in Triple Time, making two bars of one; that is to say you must observe the Rules for Triple Time on the first three crotchets of the bar, and start again on the three following, In this Signature, the accent (Mouvement) is usually marked on the first Note of each Bar composed of six Crotchets.

In six-eight time, and all Jigg mouvements, one must follow the Bow, though frequently dotted notes are met with a back Bow; only observing that in this Time Signature, whether it be a Jigg or not, if one encounters, with a back Bow, a Crotchet which is the first or third note of the Bar, one must take the following Quaver with the same Bow.

In Tunes where the Time Measure moves in Duple Time in Crotchets, you must take a forward stroke for the first part of the first and of the second Beat, T, & if the Note which begins the Bar is worth a whole Beat, you must draw the two following with a back stroke, and accent them equally, V. But if the first Note is the second or fourth part of a Beat, you must begin with a backward stroke X.

In four-eight Time, you must observe the same bowing Rules on the Quavers, as you have observed on the Crotchets in other Duple Time Measures. When the Quavers are much mixed with Semi-quavers, you must follow the Bow [i.e. let it take its course].

In all Time Signatures where the movement is not marked, & where there is no coulé or appoggiatura in the melody the bow should be allowed to take its course on equal Notes, but particularly in quick movements.

When one meets a syncopated Note with a back stroke, the following Note must be taken with the same stroke, unless this is a second syncopation; for then you must follow the Bow. This Rule must be observed particularly in Quick Movements Y.

In four-time the Quavers should be played equally, that is to say *not marking any: but with regard to Semi-quavers you should accent slightly the first, third, &c.*

For Duple Time, in quick Movements in Quavers, one should slightly mark the first, third, &c. of each Bar; but being careful not to mark them too harshly.

In Triple Time, in Quavers, you should mark a little the first of each Bar & let the others follow evenly: The same thing must be done in six-four time on the Crotchets, in quick moving Airs.

The above translation is an attempt to convey Rousseau's meaning whilst conserving his style. Occasionally the second has to give way to the first. In some cases interpretation is required, as Rousseau uses the same word to convey different ideas. For instance, " Mouvement," generally used to mean " Tempo," in some cases signifies a quick Tempo, and in yet another merely the time signature.

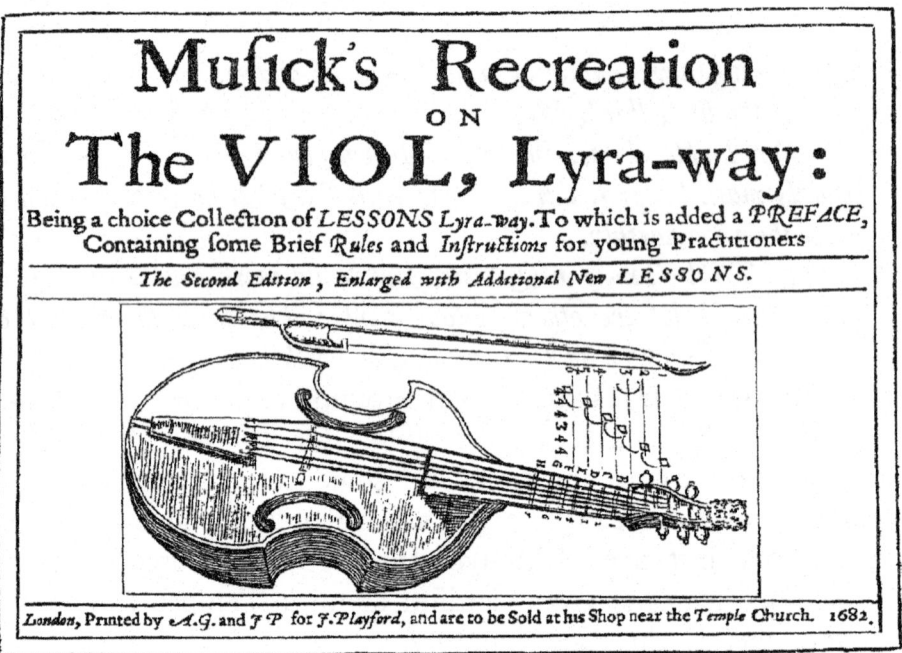

PLATE No 21
CHAPTER No 7

John Playford ' Musick Recreation on the Viol, Lyra-way,' 1682

This demonstrates how to identify the frets by letters, for playing from tablature

1

Short and *easie* Lessons *or* Tunes *for the* LYRA VIOL.

PLATE No. 22
CHAPTER No 7   Music for the Lyra Viol in tablature (John Playford, 1682)

A CHEST OF VIOLS FROM THE DOLMETSCH WORKSHOPS, HASLEMERE (1960)

CHAPTER V

THE VIOLA DA GAMBA AS A SOLO INSTRUMENT

FROM about 1600 to 1750 the viola da gamba (or bass viol, as it was more commonly called in England) was one of the most highly considered instruments for solo playing. For this reason, it has an immense repertoire, drawn from all the countries of Europe. That of the treble is also considerable, but the tenor, though it makes an attractive solo instrument, has to turn either to works for the bass which do not drop below the bottom G, or to music transposed to suit its range. The resources of the bass extend from the pieces published in tablature by Tobias Hume in 1605, to the sonatas of J. S. Bach, and even later. For the treble, there is a great deal of late seventeenth century music, chiefly French and English.

The technique of the viol differs from that of any other stringed instrument and to obtain satisfactory results the player must realise the following facts. Each viol is of much thinner and slighter construction than its nearest counterpart in the violin family, i.e., violin, viola or 'cello. To accord with this, the bridge is proportionately lower, and the strings thinner. This reduces the pressure on the belly, and results in each note having a very long vibration. Correspondingly, the viol's " underhand " bowing gives the lighter action to suit these factors, provided the wrist remains relaxed, and is moved correctly. The tone of the viol has to be drawn out with an avoidance of effort, except for the giving of an accent when required, by a brief pressure of the finger on the hair.

Rousseau, in speaking of accompanying lively music with strongly marked accents remarks that, nevertheless:

—one must not be harsh with the instrument, which requires to be treated much as one treats a horse; for if it is forced too much it takes the bit between its teeth and does not obey, on the contrary, if it is excited with moderation, one draws from it all the service one can wish. Similarly when the viol is treated harshly it gives much less tone, & often only produces a disagreable noise, whereas if one animates it without forcing the bow, it yields a beautiful tone which satisfies. One must observe the same thing in all styles of playing.

With regard to the accented stroke beginning at the point of the bow, Simpson instructs his readers as follows:

When you see an even Number of Quavers or Semi-quavers, as 2, 4, 6, 8. You must begin with your Bow forward; yea, though the Bow were employed forward in the next Note before them. But if the Number be odd, as 3, 5, 7 (which alwayes happens by reason of some Prick-note [dotted-note] or odd rest); the first of that odd number must be played with the Bow backward, This is the most proper motion of the Bow, though not absolutely without some exception: for sometimes the quickness of the Notes may force the contrary—Also quick Notes skipping from the Treble to the Bass, and so persued, are best express'd with contrary Bows.

On this vital matter of bowing there is another essential point which Simpson explains.

And, as I have formerly admonish'd you, to practise your examples first slow and then faster by degrees, that admonition is most requisite in Swift Division, where also you must be careful that the motion of your Bow and Fingers do equally answer each other, bearing your Bow moderately stiff upon the Strings [that is, not pressing too hard] at a convenient distance from the point thereof; by which you shall make your swiftest Notes most distinguishable: A thing in which many fail, either through want of a due compliance [yielding] of the Bow to the Strings or not crossing them at a right distance from the Bridge, or else by playing them too near the point of the Bow; which errors I note that you may avoyd them.

Among these useful " admonitions." the one which no other

writer mentions is that of not playing the quick notes at the point of the bow. The reason for this particular advice is that these fast notes are performed with the wrist. When the bow is at the point, the hand is thrown back to its fullest extent, and quick wrist action from this position causes the bow to jump on the string. As the full movement of which the wrist is capable is not required for these rapid passages, the player, starting from the middle to two-thirds of the bow, can conveniently use the middle-to-forward action of his wrist (the most important, and difficult to acquire), and with this the bow lies nicely on the string and the wrist is at its most relaxed.

A further useful practice in performing skipping passages from the treble strings to the bass, or the bass to the treble, is to employ a turn of the wrist to get round the strings. When starting from the bass, the bow is tipped downwards towards the bridge (even more than usual) on the edge of the hair, and then brought round almost on to the flat of the hair, on the upper string, and so back and forth. This saves considerable arm movement.

Thomas Mace is very helpful concerning the niceties of bowing to suit the viol and the occasion. He has been previously quoted as to the distance of the bow from the bridge. This is not only a matter of the size of the viol, for the reader is instructed:

2dly. According to Its Stringing, viz. If it be Stiff Strung, or Stand at High Pitch (which is both one) then Play a little Further from the Bridge.

3dly. According to Its Use, viz. If for Consort Use Play nearer the Bridge, than when you Play Alone; which although It be not so Sweet, yet It is more Lusty, and a little Ruffness is lost in the Crowd; so likewise you may do if you be to Play at a Great Distance from the Auditors, for the same Reason; for the Ruffness will be lost before it come at Them: But if you be to Play very near your Auditors, especially unto Curious Ears, Play a little too far off, rather than too near; for by that means, your Play will be the more Sweet, &c.

With regard to the left-hand technique, open strings are used indiscriminately with stopped ones, except where vibrato is required, the frets making the tone much the same. In the seventeenth century the vibrant tone of the open string appears to have been treated as one of the desirable qualities of the viol, as is to be seen in the quantity of music written in tablature, and also in the fingerings of Simpson, Marais and Forqueray. For added vibration, stopped notes were sometimes played in unison with the open string, at important points in the music. Matthew Locke's system was to mark such notes by giving them two tails. An examination of notes thus marked will show that they are always such as can be played on an open string.

In the eighteenth century, the practice appears to have developed, among certain players, of playing whole passages upon one string.

This practice [says Hubert le Blanc, in 1740] *proceeds only from ignorance of the fingerboard, as by subjecting yourself to playing on the same string as much as possible you produce only one thread of sound, beautiful in truth but giving the effect of one line.*

Thomas Mace and Simpson speak of the importance of holding down notes with the left hand after the bow has left them; this, of course, can only be done when playing across the strings. The advantage of these " holds " is that the note continues to vibrate after the bow has left the string, thus providing some of the harmonies of the piece; the ear unconsciously picks up the under-current of sounds, and is not left with the " one thread of sound " objected to by le Blanc. The rediscovery of this earlier principle of viol technique, which he considers " new," leads him to write as follows:

The new method, on the contrary, proves that to command three strings, which one keeps in mind the whole time, placing the fingers thereon simultaneously, gives a semblance of a spray of water, affording one the power of producing notes with the speed of Cossoni [*a celebrated*

Italian singer] *and over and above permitting one to play several notes at once.*

In holding down the strings simultaneously, the passage of notes from one to another is less perceptible than if one hovers, while shifting the hand, over one particular string, of which one becomes the slave for the resulting quality of tone. The hand will not form itself when limited to the greater portion of one string as having more vibration: whereas holding several strings firmly against the fingerboard, one learns to draw almost as much tone as from an open string. One avoids these Niagara-like leaps, so ungraceful to see in the carriage of the hand, which imply an ignorance of the fingerboard and an obstacle to connected notes, *that is to say with the sequence of a kind of* slur *caused by the bow finding the strings ready pressed to receive it, as are produced by the voice of Cossoni; uniting in one woven tissue the many notes she can produce with a single breath.*

It must not be imagined that in the shifting of the hand one is only considering grace, but rather the union of sounds contained within a phrase, like words between full-stops and even commas, where it is permissible for a voice to take a breath; and in the same fashion on the viol, to pass from one position, which has lasted one phrase, to another which will last as long. There will result from this a declamation such as from Le Couvreur, Melle More [singers?] *or* Forcroi le Père [Antoine Forqueray] *on the viol. Here then is this formulated maxim. The shifting of the hand at the right moment has the same effect as to breathe, when the sense of a phrase permits it without interruption.*

(In consequence one must teach the viol as one does the harpsichord to the ladies, making each change of hand accord with the musical phrase taking a new direction.) Have in mind three or four notes at once, placing the fingers in so many Niches. *The work of the left hand depends on the knowledge of four different places where one can place the fingers to play the same passage, which makes the fingerboard, in consequence, four times as difficult to get into one's mind as the keyboard of the harpsichord.*

The position to choose, out of the four, is determined by the facility with which one passes from one phrase to the one following, the ease of playing which interrupts least the thread of the Musical Discourse, and the link between its phrases, is the compass which serves as a guide in choosing a position.

One must play according to the composer's intentions: if it is at the base of the neck hold yourself there firmly, proudly, and with assurance, for to descend and ascend incessantly is to make terms with Heaven and Hell. No man can serve two masters at once.

On the subject of " holds," Rousseau asserts that there are two kinds, the first intended to maintain a good position of hand, and the second to sustain the harmonies of the piece.

Thomas Mace considers the neglect of the " holds " with the left hand, to be a gross fault:

And I will take the more Pains to Explain the Error; because It is the Grossest that can be Committed in the Kind.

And that you may know the right meaning of a Hold, Observe: the Best Lessons [pieces] of the Best Masters are often so Compos'd as They shall seem to be Single, and very Thin Things, viz. All Single Letters [notes], without any Full Stops [chords], &c. Yet upon a Judicious Examination, there will be found a Perfect Composition, of an Intire Bass, and Treble: with Strong Intimations of Inner Parts.

To many string players and singers, the idea that a plain note, without vibrato, can be beautiful, will seem strange; though there are others who are well aware of it. Vibrato on the viol was used only occasionally, to express emotion and to heighten an effect. Used thus sparingly its power is much increased.

A mode of expression which was much favoured on the viol was the swelling of the note, either with or without vibrato. Musical phrases were also swelled and diminished, as here described by Hubert le Blanc:

The grace of Musical Discourse consists in making the appropriate decrease [of volume] follow the Increase, as in the well-formed leg of a Lady, which the Queen of Navarre held to have such power over the heart of Man. The swell is employed in each direction in which the musical phrase finishes. One softens the conjunctions, which played alone would have no meaning, and serve only as a link.

Marais has a sign for the swelled note (as well as two for different kinds of vibrato), placing a little " e " above the note, with an added " p " when he wants the swelling only on the dot of a dotted note.

In the five books of " Pièces de Violes " by Marin Marais, there are to be found many signs for ornaments and graces. Those for vibrato are placed at intervals in slow, tender or passionate music. The analysis of a phrase in a piece of this character will show that the chief points of expression lie in one or two notes. If these are given vibrato or swelled, or both, the passage springs to life in a way that would be impossible if it were done to every note.

Marais' two kinds of vibrato are the only ones on record as having been used on the viol, with the exception of an " organ-shake " played with the bow, the frequent use of which was not, in Simpson's opinion " much commendable." The first one is performed with two fingers pressed together (the finger already required for the note with the next one added to it), one finger resting behind the fret whilst the other is brought down to touch the string repeatedly, in front of the fret, by a rapid rocking of the wrist, " so softly and nicely " says Simpson, " that it makes no variation of tone." For the information that the fingers must be pressed together, which in its turn makes it clear that the movement is a hand-and-wrist one, we are indebted to Rousseau, the most detailed of our sources. The second type of vibrato, similarly performed with the wrist, is for the little finger only, or for double-stops, when the fingers are on two strings. The two kinds of vibrato described by Rousseau are identical with those of Marais, though he names them differently. He explains that the second type is to supplement the first, which is not possible when stopping a note with the little finger. In Rousseau's opinion, vibrato could be used in all kinds of play, that is to say in melodic and harmonic solo playing, when accompanying one's own voice with the viol, or when playing in a group of mixed instruments; these being the various classes of music that he lists in his book. He states that it can never make a bad effect, and is particularly agreeable in a tender piece. Simpson mentions only the first type of vibrato, as does Playford. It should be stated that for the second kind, the little finger has to balance well on the fret for it to be effective.

A paragraph from Simpson will give an idea of what was expected in the matter of " expression " on the viol. At the close of his table of Graces he adds:

Of these fore-mentioned Graces, some are more rough and Masculine, as your Shaked Beats and Back-falls, and therefore more peculiar to the Bass; Others, more smooth and Feminine, as your Close-shake and plain Graces, which are more natural to the Treble, or upper parts. Yet when we would express Life, Courage, or Cheerfulness upon the Treble, we do frequently use both Shaked Beats and Backfalls, as on the contrary, smooth and swelling Notes when we would express Love, Sorrow, Compassion, or the like; and this not only on the Treble, but sometimes also on the Bass. And all these are concerned in our Division-Viol, as imploying the whole Compass of the Scale, and acting by turns all the Parts therein contained.

DOLMETSCH FAMILY CONSORT, HASLEMERE (1925)
led by Arnold Dolmetsch

Photograph by Francois Dolmetsch

PLATE No 24

1. 2. 3. Vioin de Gamba.   4. Viol Baftarda.   5. Italianifche Lyra de bracio.

Praetorius 'Syntagma Musicum' (1640)

*

CHAPTER VI

ORNAMENTATION AND INTERPRETATION
ON THE VIOL

IT is now widely accepted that an essential to the performance
of music of the sixteenth, seventeenth and eighteenth centuries
is a thorough knowledge of the conventions of ornamentation
and interpretation of the period.   The further one goes back into
the past, the more one is faced with the bare bones of great music.
Those familiar with the extravagant elaborations of Eastern
music, which have been learned by ear from player to player
down the generations, can imagine what this would be reduced
to if it were limited to the mere ground-work on which this
filigree of sound is founded.

A great deal of the manner of performance in the sixteenth
to eighteenth centuries was the same for all instruments then in
use; some ornaments, however, are individual to the viol, and
considerable information is available on the subject from writers
for that instrument.

French writers and composers are particularly detailed in
this matter, in contrast to the English, who are somewhat sparing.
Thus Marais gives in his prefaces, a series of signs for ornaments
and expression for, as he says in his third book:

> *The most beautiful pieces lose infinitely of their charm if they are
> not played in the style proper to them, and being unable to give an idea of
> this style by ordinary notes, I have been obliged to supplement with new
> signs capable of making those who play my pieces enter into my wishes.*

A matter of interpretation which can affect the whole
character of the music is that of playing apparently even notes,

63

unevenly. That this was customary is made quite clear by Marais, in the following remarks:

The dots which are above unslurred notes signify that they should be played, each note, equal, whereas one dots them usually, from the first to the second: and when they are not so marked, in these kinds of movements, one can nevertheless play them as though they were [that is, even], *as the style of the piece will sometimes call for it naturally, as in the Allemandes* [processional German dances of a marchlike character] *which do not require this observation, and I have only marked them* [the dots] *in those places which might be in doubt and even in the figured basses; these dots are much in use among foreigners.*

Strangely enough, this manner of treating even notes has survived, by a process of export to South America by the early settlers, to be handed down through generations of musicians and finally to return to us with the popularity of South American jazz.

Francois Couperin, in " L'Art de Toucher le Clavecin " (1717) deplores the inaccuracy of writing notes even, when they are to be played uneven. Johann Joachim Quantz, whose book on the transverse flute was published in 1752, informs us of the convention by which notes slurred in pairs were played uneven. Among English musicians there is the possibility that the slur was, very occasionally, used with the same intention. A few slurred pairs are to be found in Simpson's " Division Viol," in places where uneven notes would render the phrase more expressive, and as he does not even slur his written-out trills (though explaining in earlier instructions that they should be played with one stroke of the bow) it may well be assumed that this was his intention. Similar slurs occur also with other seventeenth century composers.

For the fact that uneven notes were often written even, there is the evidence of duplicate manuscripts of William Lawes and others, one giving even notes and the other dotted.

Dynamics were seldom indicated, but were generally left to the taste of the player. Simpson gives us the following information:

Gracing of Notes is performed two wayes, viz by the Bow, and by the fingers. By the Bow, as when we play Loud or Soft, according to our fancy, or the humour of the Musick. Again, this Loud or Soft is sometimes expres'd in one and the same Note, as when we make it Soft at the Beginning, and then (as it were) swell or grow louder towards the middle or ending.

In speaking of two viols extemporising divisions together, he suggests that they may:

Joyn together in a Thundering Strain of Quick Division; with which they may conclude; or else with a Strain of Slow and Sweet Notes, according as may best sute the circumstance of time and place.

Slurs in the modern sense of the word, were carefully marked by Marais, and so arranged that the accents were always on the forward stroke. His slurrings are most valuable, both in playing works of his own and in interpreting those of others. Rousseau also marks slurs in his examples in the " Traité de la Viole."

Simpson describes their use among the bowed " Graces ":

To these may be added that of Playing two, three, four or more Notes with one Motion of the Bow, which would not have that Grace or ornament if they were played severally.

From this it can be realised that slurs should be added to the English music where taste and a knowledge of the style suggest them, though they were not generally marked by the composers. In this respect a study of the indications of the French masters is helpful, taken in conjunction with Simpson's words.

That unisons were both intended and indicated by composers is also made clear in a paragraph in Simpson's " Division Viol ":

Where you see any Note with a Tail both upward and downward —it signifies two Strings sounding in Unison; one being stopped and the other open.

This is an indication frequently to be found in the bass duos of Matthew Locke.

Simpson also gives a table of what he calls " Graces to be performed with the fingers, with their signs and manner of performance," for which he tells us he is indebted to " The ever famous Charles Colman Doctor in Musick." Playford also makes use of Colman's table, though without acknowledgement. The signs themselves are of little use as he and the other English writers practically never use them; the explanations, however, are most valuable, with their detailed representation of the ornaments required in seventeenth century music.

The *Agréments* (as the French call the ornaments) are, according to Rousseau:

A melodic salt which seasons the melody, and which gives it the flavour, without which it would be tasteless and insipid, & which like salt must be used with prudence, in such that neither too much nor too little is required, & that more is required in the seasoning of certain meats and less in others : Thus in using ornaments one must apply them with moderation, & be able to discern where more are required and where less.

In another passage he states:

In quick ("leger") and accented movements, ornaments must be few.

According to Joachim Quantz, in his " Essai d'une Methode pour apprendre à jouer de la Flute Traversière," which was published in Berlin in 1752 (in a German and in a French edition) the Germans were less given to ornamentation than the other nations, being chiefly limited to simple trills at the cadences:

Except that they filled-in, here and there, intervals which involved a leap, with running notes.

Quantz was speaking, in this case, of previous times. In his own time, he tells us, German taste was beginning to be affected by Italian influences. Of the Italian style, however, Quantz did not approve:

The Italian manner of playing is arbitrary, extravagant, artificial, obscure, very often too bold and strange and difficult of performance; it admits of adding many ornaments, and assuming a considerable knowledge of harmony, it excites in those who have it not more astonishment than pleasure. The French manner of playing is slavish, but modest, clear, neat and appropriate in the expression, easy to imitate, neither precious nor obscure, intelligible to everyone and convenient for amateurs; it does not require a great knowledge of harmony, the greater part of the ornaments being set-down by the composer; but on the other hand, it does not give the connoisseurs much to think out.

Quantz draws the conclusion that the French music depends more on the composition and the Italian on the performance; which is to state that the French wrote out their intentions far more fully than the Italians, who depended more on the interpretation of the performer. He adds further:

The manner of singing of the Italians is preferable to their manner of playing; and the manner of playing of the French is preferable to their manner of singing.

Allowance must be made for the fact that Quantz writes in 1752, when ornamentation, particularly in Italy, had become somewhat extravagant.

Rousseau explains the ornaments fully, though he has, quite unnecessarily, given them names of his own. Fortunately, he explains his meaning in terms of the generally accepted nomenclature in France.

The names (and their signification) which the player will find of the most practical use are those given by Simpson, correlated to those of Marais. Marais' signs are important as they were, basically, those in general use in France, added to by himself.

THE ORNAMENTS

Swelled Note. (Marais: "enflé," sign "e," or "e p.", if the swelling is on the dot of a dotted note).

Plain Beat or Rise. (Marais has no sign).

A kind of upward appoggiatura, used when rising a tone or a semi-tone; the first note is repeated before a slurred rise to the second, taking up a part of its value.

Back-fall. (Written-out by Marais.)

This is a similar appoggiatura, but descending.

Elevation. (Marais " Coulé," sign " ∕ .")

A form of " coulé," performed by sliding up to a note from the third below (or sometimes the fifth). The little notes added to this take together half the value of the lower written note.

Double-Back-fall. (Written-out by Marais.)

Same as the *elevation*, but downwards, the time value of the little notes being taken from that of the upper written note.

Acute or Springer. (Written-out by Marais.)

Performed by clapping down a finger at the expiration of a note, thus raising it a tone or a semitone for a short fraction of time. Rousseau says it should be used before a trill with appoggiatura, and can be performed, alternately with such trills, several times in succession.

Cadent. (Written-out by Marais.)

When descending a tone or a semitone, the second note is anticipated at the close of the first, taking up part of its time value.

All the preceding ornaments come under the heading of what Simpson calls " Smooth Graces." The following are the " Shaked Graces," under which heading he classes trills, mordents and vibrato.

Close Shake. (Marais " Pincé ou Flatement," sign " ∿ .")

This is the vibrato performed with two fingers pressed close together, by a sideways rocking of the wrist, as previously described.

Plainte. (Given by Marais and Rousseau, sign " ⸾ .")

The vibrato performed with the little finger balanced on the fret, by a rocking of the wrist. It is also used occasionally for double-stops, the two fingers being balanced on the frets.

The Back-fall Shaked.   (Marais " Tremblement," sign " , " after the note).
Trill with appoggiatura.

Batement.   (Given by Marais and Rousseau, sign " x ", before the note.)
This is a mordent; i.e., play the written note, then down a tone or semitone and up again.

Shaked Beat.   (For this Marais adds a little note to his " Batement " sign.)
A kind of mordent, trilling the Plain Beat previously described.

Shaked Elevation.   (Marais indicates this with combined signs and notes.)
In this is combined a " coulé " of a third, with a beat on the top note and a turn at the close.

Shaked Cadent and Double Relish.
This combination of ornaments will be better understood by a study of Simpson's table than by a verbal explanation.

An idea of the universal use of a trill at a close can be obtained from the following passage from Simpson's " Compendium of Practical Musick " (1665).   He is discussing how to overcome the imperfections of the tempered scale from the intonation angle:

Only one place there is where I conceive a Quarter-note might serve instead of a semi-tone; which is in the binding Cadence of the greater (major) third and that, commonly, is drowned either by the Trill of the voice or the Shake of the finger.

This paragraph, besides making the point for which it was quoted, also shows that the refinements of intonation were studied and sought after, and that the trill of the voice and the shake of the finger were musically synonymous.

Speaking of ornamentation in accompaniment and ensemble playing, Rousseau says:

The spirit of accompaniment demands that if some ornament is made in a certain phrase of the melody, and that same phrase should recur afterwards in the other parts, after the manner of a fugue or imitation, one should make the same ornament as was made the first time.

The spirit of accompaniment requires, in fact, that if one hears the treble make some ornament or slur on a particular phrase of the melody, the bass should do likewise when it imitates the same phrase.

Speaking of the treble viol, Rousseau states:

The playing of melody is the proper character of the Treble Viol, rather than the playing of pieces in harmony, which is why those who wish to play it well should attach themselves to all the delicacy of the melody, to imitate all that a beautiful Voice can do with all the charms of Art—

One should use all the ornaments to their full extent, particularly the "Cadence avec Appuy" [Simpson's Back-fall Shaked] *and the "Port de Voix"* [Simpson's Plain Beat] *which are the foundations of Melody, and one must not omit in one's playing anything which can give pleasure to the ear with strokes both tender and rich.*

Rousseau, however, warns the player to avoid a profusion of passages which only confuse the melody, and which he says are called "faire des colifichets," as also he must practise those passages from the top to the bottom, and from the bottom to the top of the instrument which are called " ricochets "

and which one barely endures in violin playing, but all the graces and passages [elaboration of phrases] *must be natural and used "a propos" and with wit—*

One must beware, according to Rousseau, of marking the accents too much in lively music, lest one depart from the character of the treble viol

which does not require to be treated like the Violin, whose function is to animate, whereas that of the treble viol is to flatter.

In the example given of Rousseau's ornamentation, it will be observed that he uses a small cross to indicate a trill; this was a common practice. Some composers used this cross as a universal

XXI

1. 2. Kleine Poschen / Geigen ein Octav höher. 3. Discant-Geig ein Quart höher.
4. Rechte Discant-Geig. 5. Tenor-Geig. 6 Bas-Geig de bracio. 7. Trumscheit.
8. Scheidtholtt.

Praetorius ' Syntagma Musicum ' (1640)

1. Clavicymbel, so eine Quart tieffer alß Chor-Thon.   2. Octav-Posaun.   3. Groß Doppel Quint-Posaun.   4. Violone, Groß Viol-de Gamba-Baß.

Praetorius 'Syntagma Musicum' (1640)

sign that an ornament was required, leaving it to the player to supply the suitable grace.

Finally, in the words of Rousseau:

It must be observed that all ornaments which alter the time measure of the " Mouvement " [mood or style] *should never be used.*

CHAPTER VII

THE VIOL PLAYED "LYRA WAY"

IN the reign of Elizabeth I a new member was added to the family of viols in England: the Lyra or Harp Viol.

The ancestor of the lyra viol is probably to be found in an earlier Italian instrument, known as the Lyra da Gamba. This instrument was a true viol in its method of tone production, for it was fretted, bowed with the "underhand" bowing, and held between the knees like the viola da gamba. Its chief use was for accompanying the voice; with its nearly flat bridge and twelve strings, tuned in an "up and down" tuning, it lent itself readily to playing in harmony in the simpler keys.

The English court had many connections with Italy in the sixteenth century; Elizabeth herself spoke Italian fluently and brought to her court a number of Italian musicians. Of these Alfonso Ferrabosco I, who entered her service in about 1560, is credited with bringing the lyra viol to England, and Ferrabosco II, who became a fine musician and composer, was one of those who helped to popularize it. He composed works for one, two and three lyra viols, which were published in 1609. Among those for one lyra are pieces originally written by him for a consort of five viols, including his magnificent "Dovehouse Pavan." Such works stretch the resources of the instrument and the hand of the player to the utmost, and would be unplayable on a full-sized viola da gamba. The lyra of this period, however, was a comparatively small instrument, not much larger than a consort tenor.

One of the great charms of the lyra lay in the fact that it had a variable tuning, being tuned in a chord to suit the key of particular pieces; this, besides admitting of many chords and double-stops, gave a sympathetic resonance to the whole viol. To increase this as much as possible great use was made of open strings, octaves and unisons, obtained by playing on two strings at once, one being stopped by the finger to give the same note as the adjoining open string. As the tuning of the viol itself usually included a pair of octaves and fifths, the resonance achieved was very great.

Daniel Farrant, one of the early lyra composers, was said to have invented a lyra with sympathetic strings running underneath the finger-board, as in the viola d'amore. If this was really so, it seems to have been an unnecessary complication, as there is no evidence of its having been adopted by any of Farrant's contemporaries.

Another of the attractive characteristics of the lyra was the use of pizzicato notes plucked with the left hand, interspersed with the bowed notes; these were called " thumps."

There were as many as twenty-three recognized tunings for the lyra, and no doubt further variants were used by some players. Such a variety would cause confusion to modern players who, playing from staff notation, might seek their notes in the wrong places. In the sixteenth and seventeenth centuries, however, this difficulty did not exist, for composers employed tablature as for the lute, and tablature indicates not the note, but its position on the finger-board.

Notation by tablature is simple to understand, once it is realised that each line of the six-line stave represents a string, and each letter a position on the string, " a " standing for the open string, " b " the first fret, " c " the second, and so on up the finger-board; the time values being indicated above the stave.

A further advantage of tablature is that it can be played from, so long as the viol is tuned in the correct intervals, irrespective of the size and usual pitch of the viol.

Early in the seventeenth century, musicians began to discover that the system of playing and tuning the lyra could be applied to any viol, and the term playing the viol " lyra-way " came into use. The most usual member of the family to be so employed was the Division Viol, which was a little smaller than the consort bass. A proof of this development lies in the title of a publication by John Playford. In 1652 it was published as " Musick's Recreation on the Lyra Viol "; in the three subsequent editions it appeared as " Musick's Recreation on the Viol: Lyra way."

Though a great proportion of the music written was for what Playford calls " The lone Lyra Viol," there were many consorts for lyras, such as those composed by Ferrabosco II, and some also for viols played " lyra way." Tobias Hume published in 1605 pieces for " two Lyro Viols, and also for the Lyro viol with two treble viols, or two with one treble." The music is entirely in tablature, the treble parts being for viols tuned in the same intervals as the lyra, but an octave higher. This, perhaps, was the kind of consort which Thomas Mace had in mind when, in " Musick's Monument " (1676) he describes the ideal music room and its furnishings. After listing in detail the " Chest of Viols," a pair of violins, and another of theorbo lutes, which should grace the room he continues:

And now, to make your store more Amply-Compleat, add to all these 3 Full seiz'd Lyro Viols; there being most Admirable Things made by our Very Best Masters, for that Sort of Musick, both Consort-wise, and peculiarly for two and three Lyroes.

Let them by Lusty, Smart-Speaking Viols; because in Consort they often retort against the Treble; imitating and often standing instead of That Part, viz., a Second Treble.

That music was written for lyras in combination with other instruments is, however, also a fact. When Thomas Britton, the famous " musical small coal man " died in 1714, his library contained eighteen sets of books of lyra consorts, including some in 2, 3, 4 and 5 parts by John Jenkins, eight sets described as for lyra, violin and bass (probably continuo gamba and harpsichord).

Of the many tunings with which the lyra began its life in England, some were very extended, there being as much as two octaves and a fourth between the first and the sixth string. With the passage of time these extreme tunings fell out of use as they were impracticable with the usual viol stringing. The later editions of Playford are restricted to two tunings, those known as " Harp-way Sharp " and " Harp-way Flat " providing a major and a minor tuning.

Playford's recipe for setting the pitch of the lyra is to tune the top string " as high as it will go without breaking," and from this by intervals, the rest of the strings. This perilous proceeding must have led to varying results according to the courage of the player. It also makes it quite clear that, for the " lone lyra," the pitch was not considered important.

One anonymous seventeenth century MS. gives us an indication as to the pronunciation of the name " lyra." The three-part pieces which it contains are described as " Leero-sett," showing that the " y " must have been pronounced short, like the " i " in give.

Among the numerous composers who wrote for the lyra and the viol played lyra way, besides those already mentioned, were such well-known men as William Corkine, Giovanni Coperario, William Lawes, Christopher Simpson, Simon Ives and William Young.

In addition to the original works of such composers, a vast number of popular tunes and songs were set, or turned into fantasias for the instrument, giving proof of the popularity of playing the viol in this fashion in the seventeenth century.

CHAPTER VIII

THE CONSORT OF VIOLS

AT the time of Henry VII wind instruments predominated considerably over strings in this country, and it is not till the reign of Henry VIII that one can trace the development of the consort for viols, from the vocal part-music of the churches on the one side, and the instrumental dance music on the other. Henry himself, musician and composer, had twenty-five viols in his collection when he died, though he had far more flutes, recorders and other wind instruments.

Development after this was swift, and by the time Elizabeth I was on the throne, consort music for viols was fully established. Thomas Morley in his " Plaine and Easie Introduction to Practicall Musick " (1597) speaks of it as follows:

> *The most principal and chiefest kind of music which is made without a dittie is the fantasie, that is when a musician taketh a point at his pleasure, and wresteth and turneth it as he lists, making either much or little of it as shall seem best in his own conceit. In this may be shown more art than in any other music, because the composer is tied to nothing but that he may add, diminish and alter at his pleasure. And this will bear any allowances whatsoever tolerable in other kinds of music, except changing the ayre and leaving the key, which in fantasie may never be suffered. Other things you may use at your pleasure, as bindings with discords, quick motions, slow motions, proportions, and what you list.*

Fifty years later, even those few restrictions which Thomas Morley placed on the fantasy had been swept aside.

The viol as an instrument is particularly suited to contra-puntal music, its thin reedy tone, with the clarity of a fretted instrument, helping the individual parts to follow their separate ways whilst remaining distinct one from another, in spite of their constant crossing and overlapping. This quality of the viol must have contributed considerably to the development of the fantasy.

In the 17th century, many big houses had their chests of viols, and visitors would drop in on the recognized night of that particular household, to bear a part with members of the family in fantasies (or fancies as they were sometimes called), pavans or other ensemble works, those present taking their turn as players or listeners according to the number of callers at this particular musical " at home."

Speaking of furnishing the music room, Thomas Mace writes in 1676:

Your best provision (and most complete) will be a Good Chest of Viols; Six in number; viz. 2 Basses, 2 Tenors, and 2 Trebles: All truly and Proportionately Suited.

Alternatively, the first tenor can be replaced by an alto, tuned c to c″. Even in the case of such an instrument being tuned like the tenor (Ganassi tuning), the smaller viol would have a different colour of tone and be richer in its upper register; the string length of all stringed instruments being always a compromise as, ideally, the higher strings should be proportionately shorter than the lower ones.

After theorising as to the reasons for which a viol improves with age, Mace continues:

Now, suppose you cannot procure an Intire Chest of Viols Suitable &c. Then Thus.

Endeavour to Pick up (Here, or There) so many excellent Good odd ones, as near Suiting as you can (every way), viz. both for Shape, Wood, Colour, &c. but especially for Scize.

And to be Exact in That, take this Certain Rule, viz. Let your Bass be Large. Then your Trebles must be just as Short again, in the String (viz.) from Bridge, to Nut, as are your Basses; because they stand 8 Notes Higher than the Basses; Therefore as Short again; for the Middle of Every String, is an 8th. The Tenors (in the String) just so long as from the Bridge, to F Fret [the 5th fret in tablature]; *because they stand a 4th Higher, than your Basses; Therefore so Long.*

One of the great advantages of consort music is that works can be found to suit almost any combinations of viols from two to seven. This means that as soon as two players meet they can form their consort, and stand as an encouragement to others, who are tempted to join them after a time. To quote Mace again:

—we had Those Choice Consorts, to Equally-Sciz'd Instruments (Rare Chests of Viols), and as equally Perform'd: For we would never Allow Any Performer to Over-top, or Out-cry another by Loud Play; but our Great Care was, to have all the Parts Equally Heard; by which means (though sometimes we had but indifferent, or mean Hands to Perform with) yet This Caution made the Musick Lovely, and very Contentive.

The equality between the parts is one of the great charms of this kind of music; it is spoken of by many writers and stressed several times by Mace.

Of the thousands of existing compositions there are works to suit every degree of proficiency, from the complete beginner to the brilliant virtuoso, and with the added advantage that the easiest consorts are quite as great musically as the most difficult. The first essential is, as always, that the player should have control of wrist and bow and therefore produce a pleasant free tone in slow notes. Such a player is then able to play the theme in notes lasting a bar each, in an " In Nomine " fantasy, whilst the more skilled performers weave their patterns around this vital central thread.

It is interesting to remember that it was Arnold Dolmetsch's accidental discovery at the British Museum of fantasies for viols, whilst he was searching for viola d'amore music, which inspired him to devote his life to the restoration of ancient music and instruments, his first " modern " performance of fantasies being given in 1891.

The question of ornamentation in consort playing is one on which the English writers give us little guidance. Whilst ornaments used to excess would obviously obscure contrapuntal passages, there is no reason to suppose that they were barred, especially from closes. Christopher Simpson, in his brilliant suites for one treble and two bass viols, fills the Fantasy with as many written-out trills and ornaments as he does the Ayre and Galliard which complete each suite, and though these fantasies are less contrapuntal than the usual consorts for the " Chest of Viols " they are nevertheless related. There exist, besides, certain part-books and score-books in which the scribe has written, in margins or on odd pages, various embellishments and floridly ornamented closes which appear to have been meant as a guide to himself, for performance in consort after private study. Rousseau gives us a clue as to French practice when several instruments were playing together, by telling us that if a certain phrase is ornamented by one player, and later recurs in another part after the manner of a fugue, it should be similarly ornamented. The conclusion appears to be that a discreet " Gracing " of parts is not out of place.

In the performance of consorts, if rhythm and phrasing, cross-rhythm and cross-phrasing are to make their effect, a more detached style of playing is demanded than would be required of a string quartet, because of the long resonance of the viols. A particularly helpful point to observe is the shortening and detaching of the leading note. It is a safe rule that, while remaining aware of the other moving parts, each player must declaim and accent his own phrase according to its rhythmic requirements, even though it should occur at one beat's distance in canon with another part.

Dynamics are also controlled by the polyphonic nature of the music, each part rising as it has something of importance to say, and making way for another when this in turn receives the theme. There are generally, however, passages where the viols come together for a short while, and here fine contrasts of tone can be effectively employed, from a passionate forte to a tender pianissimo; while some contrapuntal sections will need to be altogether gentler and softer than others. Though most fantasies will rise to a climax or grand conclusion in the last few bars, the final note is never held fortissimo and cut off abruptly at the end, but is rather allowed to diminish and finish softly, on the principle that, according to Hubert le Blanc, a note on the viol is not, as on the violin, part of a column of sound capable of being moulded but is like a stroke of the great bell of St. Germain which dies away on the air.

Of the works for viols, Simpson speaks as follows, in his " Compendium of Practical Musick " (London, 1665):

We must now speak a little more of music made for instruments; in which points, fugues and all other Figures of Descant are in no less (if not in more) use than in vocal music.

Of this kind the chief and most excellent, for art and contrivance, are Fancies, of 6, 5, 4 and 3 parts, intended commonly for viols. In this sort of music the composer (being not limited to words) doth employ all his art and invention solely about the bringing in and carrying on of these fugues, according to the order and method formerly shewed.

When he has tried all the several ways which he thinks fit to be used therein; he takes some other Point, and does the like with it: or else, for variety, introduces some chromatic notes, with bindings and intermixtures of discords; or falls into some lighter humour like a Madrigal, or what his own fancy shall lead him to: but still concluding with something which hath Art and Excellency in it.

Of this sort you may see many compositions made heretofore in England by Alfonso Ferrabosco, Coperario, Lupo, White, Ward, Mico, Dr. Colman, now deceased. Also by Mr. Jenkins, Mr. Lock, and divers other excellent men, Doctors and Batchelors in music, yet living.

The next in dignity after a Fancy is a Pavan, which some derive from Padua in Italy; at first ordained for a grave and stately manner of dancing (as most instrumental musics were in their several kinds,

Fancies and Symphonies excepted), but now grown up to a height of Composition made only to delight the ear.

Simpson concludes with the following words:

You need not seek for Outlandish Authors, especially for Instrumental Music; no Nation (in my opinion) being equal to the English in that way; as well for their excellent as their various and numerous Consorts, of 3, 4, 5 and 6 parts, made properly for instruments; of all which (as I said) Fancies are the chief.

Though in fantasies all the parts are equal, each group of players had its accustomed leader; an instance of this is to be observed in the diary of that great musical amateur Anthony Wood. He is describing the music meetings which took place at the house of William Ellis (formerly organist at Eton College) at Oxford, where many Royalist musicians had taken refuge during the " Protectorate " of Oliver Cromwell. One of those who frequented the weekly meetings was " Dr. John Wilson, the public Professor, the best at the Lute in all England. He sometimes play'd the lute but mostly presided the Consort." (This too, when the host was himself a musician.) Will Ellis, bachelor of music, we are told, " alwaies play'd his part on the organ or virginal."

It was the custom to accompany the consort with, preferably, an organ, but alternatively a virginal or lute continuo. This part was by no means restricted to sustaining chords, but would more often pick out the theme as it passed from viol to viol, as may be seen from many original organ parts.* Thomas Mace gives a very attractive picture of the function of the organ in consort. He gives a list of the best composers of fantasies, which is largely the same as Simpson's and then continues:

And these were played upon so many equal and truly sized viols; and so exactly strung, tuned, and played upon as no one part was any

---

* Some composers, notably William Lawes giving the organ occasional independent contrapuntal phrases.

impediment to the other; but still (as the composition required) by intervals each part amplified and heightened the other; the organ evenly, softly, and sweetly according to all.

On the pleasure and benefit that can be gained by playing in Consorts of Viols, the words of Thomas Mace cannot be improved upon.

We had for our grave music, fantasies of 3, 4, 5 and 6 parts, to the organ, intersposed (now and then) with some Pavins, Allmaines, solemn and sweet delightful Ayres; all which were so many Pathetical Stories, Rhetorical and Sublime discourses; Subtle and Acute Argumentations; so suitable, and agreeing to the inward, secret and intellectual faculties of the soul and mind; that to set them forth according to their true praise there are no words sufficient in language; yet what I can best speak of them shall be only to say, that they have been to myself (and many others), as Divine raptures, powerfully captivating all our unruly faculties, and affections (for the time), and disposing us to solidity, gravity and a good temper, making us capable of Heavenly and Divine influences.

'Tis pity few believe thus much; but far greater that so few know it.

THE END.

INDEX

by Nathalie Dolmetsch

ORGANISATIONS DEVOTED TO THE STUDY AND PERFORMANCE OF OLD MUSIC AND ON OLD INSTRUMENTS

AMERICAN INSTITUTE OF MUSICOLOGY

The publications of the A.I.M include scholarly editions of old music and treatises on music, published in four series. CORPUS MENSURABILIS MUSICAE, CORPUS SCRIPTORUM DE MUSICA, MUSICOLOGICAL STUDIES AND DOCUMENTS, and MISCELLANEA.

General Editor: Armen Carapetyan

Annual Journal: *Musica Disciplina*

Editors· Armen Carapetyan and Gilbert Reaney

Particulars about the publications of the A.I.M. from Hinrichsen Edition Ltd., Bach House, 10-12 Baches Street, London, N.1 and for U.S.A. from A.I.M , P.O Box 30665, Dallas 30, Texas.

AMERICAN MUSICOLOGICAL SOCIETY

for research into the byways of music history and science

Journal of the A.M.S (three times per year)

Editor-in-Chief: Charles Warren Fox

Particulars about Membership

from Eastman School of Music, Rochester 4, N.Y

DOLMETSCH FOUNDATION

for the promotion of early music and instruments, made at the Dolmetsch Workshops, in concerts and annual Festivals

Annual Journal: *The Consort*   Editor: Richard D. C Noble

Particulars about Membership from

Mrs. Angela Evans, Greenstead, Beacon Hill, Hindhead, Surrey

GALPIN SOCIETY

for the promotion of the history, construction and playing of old musical instruments

Annual Journal: *The Galpin Society Journal*   Editor: Anthony Baines

Particulars about Membership from

Eric Halfpenny, F S.A , 258 Cranbrook Road, Ilford, Essex

ROYAL MUSICAL ASSOCIATION

arranges 8-10 scholarly lectures per year.   The British representation of the INTERNATIONAL SOCIETY FOR MUSICOLOGY and the publishers of MUSICA BRITANNICA, R.M A. RESEARCH CHRONICLES, COMPLETE PURCELL EDITION

Annual Journal: *Proceedings of the R.M.A.*

Particulars about Membership from

Dr. Nigel Fortune, 44 Philip Victor Road, Handsworth, Birmingham 21

VIOLA DA GAMBA SOCIETY

for the promotion of the playing of viols in the authentic manner, organising an annual Summer School of viol playing and arranging a biennial competition for original consort music

Semi-Annual Journal: *The Viola da gamba Society Bulletin*

Editor: Miss Ruth Daniells

Particulars about Membership from

Miss M. Hales, 5 Ravenslea Road, Balham, London, S.W.12

SCHOLARLY BOOK PUBLICATIONS

An Annual on the History of Music:

MUSICA DISCIPLINA

Edited by ARMEN CARAPETYAN; Assistant Editor: GILBERT REANEY
The only periodical of its kind confined to Mediaeval and Renaissance subjects and limited strictly to research articles, inventories (with critical study and concordances) of the important manuscript sources, and the like The publication is abundantly illustrated with examples, facsimiles, transcriptions, etc., and has become an indispensable instrument of further research as well as a standard work of reference.

With an appendix, containing bibliographical and other notes
Hinrichsen Edition No. MD-2 to 17

Books on Music History:

REFERENCE MATERIALS IN ETHNOMUSICOLOGY
by Bruno Nettl

A bibliographic essay which organises, describes, and evaluates the basic books and articles on primitive, oriental and folk music.
Hinrichsen Edition No De-1612a

THE INNATE CHARACTER OF MUSIC

as revealed by Arabic authors from the IXth to XIXth Century
together with
the text and translation of the unique Arabic manuscript of Ya'qūb al-Kindī (d. *c.* 873) on the **'Ethos of Rhythm, Colour and Perfume,'** and **'Ghosts, an excursus on Arabic musical bibliographies'** to which is added
' The Religious Music of Islam '
edited, with translation and commentaries
by Henry George Farmer
Hinrichsen Edition No. 658

MUSICA NEU BERORIAETH

The Musical Notation of the Ancient Britons (A D. 1100)
Facsimile of the remarkable Robert ap Huw MS., with detailed introduction and a list of the names of the 24 measures of string music and the names of the scales. Said to contain the oldest music in Europe.
Hinrichsen Edition No. 378

ON THE INFLUENCE OF MUSIC

by Sa 'Adyah Gaon (d. 1042), the Great Jewish Philosopher
The Interpretation of the Rhythmic Modes, etc.
including an Index of Hebrew and Arabic Books
edited and transcribed by Henry G. Farmer
Hinrichsen Edition No. 697

AL-FARABI'S ARABIC-LATIN WRITINGS ON MUSIC

The Arabic texts and the XIIth Century translation into Latin, together with translation into English, and a critical commentary
by Henry G Farmer
Hinrichsen Edition No. 322 (second edition)

Books on Musical Instruments:

EUROPEAN MUSICAL INSTRUMENTS

A compact handbook, with 11 Plates, 8 Diagrams, 256 Pages
by Francis W. Galpin
Hinrichsen Edition No. De-1804 (fourth edition)

BASSOON AND DOUBLE BASSOON

A short illustrated History of their origin, development and makers
by Lyndesay G. Langwill
Hinrichsen Edition M-24

THE CLARINET

A well-planned book, a particular feature of which is its all-embracing description of the characteristics of the instrument, its history and mechanism,
by F. Geoffrey Rendall
With 60 illustrations, List of Music (500 items), Bibliography and List of Makers
Hinrichsen Edition No. De-1805 (second edition)

THE FRENCH HORN

The Evolution of the Instrument and its Technique
discussed by *R. Morley-Pegge*
With biographical notes on celebrated Horn Players of the Past, a List of Makers, Bibliography, numerous musical and other Illustrations and 5 Appendices.
Hinrichsen Edition No. De-1812

THE OBOE

An outline of the history and development of the Oboe
by Philip Bate
With biographical notes on the celebrated Oboe Players of the Past, Bibliography and numerous Illustrations.

THE RECORDER, ITS TRADITION AND ITS TASKS

by Hildemarie Peter, English translation by Stanley Godman
An exhaustive study of the instrument, its structural and acoustic principles, its technical problems and its history, the work provides a complete background for recorder players and teachers   Clearly presented and illustrated with many musical examples in the text, as well as with fingering charts, etc., and completed by a comprehensive bibliography, it is not only an aesthetic contribution, but holds the place of a handbook on its subject.
Hinrichsen Edition No. De-1192

A Treatise on the Art of Playing the Recorder and of Free Ornamentation

LA FONTEGARA by SYLVESTRO GANASSI

edited by Hildemarie Peter, English translation by Dorothy Swainson
Published in Venice in 1535, 'La Fontegara' is a carefully planned and systematic treatise of the art of playing the recorder and also a detailed tutor of how to play divisions and ornaments of a basic theme.   The book thus combines two historic aspects of practical musicianship in the XVIth Century. As an instruction book for recorder players it is unique and, inasmuch as the rhythmic conceptions and ornaments of the period are concerned, it is of compelling interest to all musicians.
Hinrichsen Edition No. De-1289

THE VIOLA DA GAMBA — ITS ORIGIN AND HISTORY
ITS TECHNIQUE AND MUSICAL RESOURCES

With many illustrations
by Nathalie Dolmetsch
Hinrichsen Edition No. 759

WAITS — WIND BAND — THE ORCHESTRAL HORN

'The Waits,' a historical study by *L. G Langwill*; 'The British Wind Band, its Rise and Progress during three Centuries' by *Harold C. Hind*; and 'The Orchestral French Horn, its Origin and Evolution' by *R Morley-Pegge*, with an Introduction by *Max Hinrichsen* With three pages of Wesley Facsimile, Reproduction of 24 Horns, and 12 further musical and other Illustrations.
Hinrichsen Edition No. S-16a

THOMAS MORLEY:
THE FIRST BOOK OF CONSORT LESSONS

for Treble and Bass Viols, Flute, Lute, Cittern and Pandora

A definitive edition of one of the great monuments of early music, reconstructed and edited with an historical Introduction and Critical Notes by *Sydney Beck*. Foreword by *Carleton Sprague-Smith*. xix, 195 pp. 9 Facsimiles and 7-colour Frontispiece, showing *Mask Music for a Wedding Feast*, about 1596. The mask in progress is accompanied by the same instrumental consort as prescribed for Morley's *Lessons*

A *New York Public Library* Publication – Peters Edition No. 6100. 10″ × 13″

PLAYFORD:
MUSICK'S RECREATION ON THE VIOL, LYRA-WAY

Facsimile reproduction of the second, enlarged edition of 1682, with a portrait of John Playford, a contemporary picture of a Viol, and an historical Introduction by *Nathalie Dolmetsch*.
Hinrichsen Edition No. 1682. xx, 58 Pages

MODERN URTEXT EDITIONS OF
ENGLISH XVIIth CENTURY
CHAMBER MUSIC

based on Arnold Dolmetsch's Interpretation
prepared by Nathalie Dolmetsch and Layton Ring

COPERARIO: FANTASY (5′)   **FERRABOSCO I: FANTASY (3½′)**

for 5 Viols or

2 Vns., Va. & 2 V'cellos   1 or 2 Vns , 1 or 2 Vas.
with or without Keyboard   & 2 V'cellos

Hinrichsen Edition No. 578a/b. Scores and Parts

THOMAS TOMKINS (1572-1656)
prepared by Harry Danks

In Nomine a 3 (4')	Pavan a 5 (5')
2 Treble & 1 Bass Viol or	5 Viols or
2 Vns. & V'cello	3 Vns., Va. & V'cello

Hinrichsen Edition No. 558a/b.   Scores and Parts

GEMINIANI (1687-1762): CHACONNE (9')
upon the Sarabande Theme from Corelli's Sonata Op. 5 No. 7
Violin & Harpsichord/Piano; Va. da gamba/V'cello ad lib.
discovered and prepared by Layton Ring
Expression and bowing marks by Jean Pougnet
Hinrichsen Edition No. 1687

JOHN JENKINS (1592-1678)
prepared by Cecily Arnold and Marshall Johnson

Aria in A (3')	Sonata a 2 in D m. (4 1/2')

Violin, Viola da gamba/V'cello and Keyboard
Va. da gamba/V'cello II ad lib.
Hinrichsen Edition No. 559a/b.   Score and Parts

HENRY PURCELL (1659-1695)
Fantasia: Three Parts upon a Ground (6')
3 Vns., Va. da gamba/V'cello; Keyboard ad lib.
transcribed and edited by Denis Stevens and Thurston Dart
Hinrichsen Edition No 220.   Score and Parts

OLD-ENGLISH TRIO SONATAS
with a new Keyboard realisation
2 Vns. & Keyboard; Va. da gamba/V'cello ad lib.
or 2 Vns. & Va. da gamba/V'cello or String Trio

Arne Nos. 2, 3, 4, 5, 7: G, Eb, F m., D, E m.

Boyce Nos. 2, 6, 8, 9, 12. F, Bb, Eb, C, G
prepared by Herbert Murrill and Stanley Sadie
Hinrichsen Edition Nos. 64, 78, 624/5, 627; 55, 733, 641/3

Buonamente ' La Monteverde '
the 2 Violins in strict canon throughout
prepared by Denis Stevens
Fingering and bowing marks by Yehudi Menuhin
Hinrichsen Edition No. 680

Handel Op. 5 A, D; E m., G; G m., F, Bb
prepared by K. Schleifer
Peters Edition No. 4630a/c

Purcell Eb, F (Golden); D, D m.; G m., Bb; A m., G m.
prepared by Waldemar Woehl and K. Schleifer
Peters Edition Nos. 4242a/b; 4649a/b
all Scores and Parts are available separately

MUSIC, LIBRARIES AND INSTRUMENTS

Editors: Unity Sherrington and Guy Oldham

Foreword by Dr. C. B. Oldman, C B., C.V.O.

Following the success of HINRICHSEN'S TENTH MUSIC BOOK: *Organ and Choral Aspects and Prospects*, the eleventh volume of this series covers the Papers read at the joint International Cambridge Congress of the IAML and the Galpin Society.   The subjects discussed are wide-ranging and of great interest to all music lovers.

A special feature of this volume of 300 Text Pages is its lavish use of illustrations – there are 170 Plates on 100 Pages.

among its contents.

in Section One:

Practical Musicology (*Sir Jack Westrup*)

in Section Two:

Panizzi and the Music Collection of the British Museum (*C B. Oldman*)
Music in Scottish Libraries (*Marie Linton*)

in Section Four:

Collections of Musical Instruments in Antwerp (*J. Douillez*)
*Les Collections privées d'instruments de musique (*G. Thibault*)

in Section Seven:

*Water Organs (*Susi Jeans*)

in Section Eight:

Some Points in the Nomenclature of Folk Instruments (*Anthony Baines*)

*The Evolution of the Cittern (*Emmanuel Winternitz*)

The International Catalogue of Music for the Lute and kindred Instruments (*Jean Jacquot*)

The Cylindrical Reed Pipe from Antiquity to the 20th Century (*James MacGillivray*)

*The Javanese Rebab (*Mantle Hood*)

*Henry Purcell's Use of the Recorder (*Walter Bergmann*)

*Shawm Band Pieces by Couperin (*Guy Oldham*)

*Musical Treasures of the Vienna Art Museum (*Victor Luithlen*)

*The Schreinzer Collection of String Instrumental Fittings (*Kenneth Skeaping*)

in Section Nine:

*Mediaeval Musical Instruments sculptured in the Decoration of English Churches (*Charles and Harriet Nicewonger*)

The American contributors (in order of the contributions): *Dr. Vincent Duckles, Dr. Harold Spivake, Rita Benton, Dr. E. Winternitz, Professor Mantle Hood, H. J. Hedlund, C. and H. Nicewonger, Professor Jan LaRue and Jeanette B. Holland.*

* with numerous illustrations.   Hinrichsen No. 1962a.   Cloth Bound

CPSIA information can be obtained at www.ICGtesting.com
Printed in the USA
BVOW09s1145080215

386835BV00007B/124/P